CLOUD COMPUTING BASICS

Understanding AWS, Azure, and Google Cloud

THOMPSON CARTER

TABLE OF CONTENTS

INTRODUCTION

The cloud has revolutionized the way technology powers our lives, businesses, and innovations. Once seen as a futuristic concept, cloud computing has become an indispensable backbone for industries ranging from healthcare to finance, from education to retail, and beyond. As businesses shift away from traditional on-premises infrastructure to adopt cloud solutions, the demand for skilled professionals who can navigate and harness the power of the cloud has skyrocketed. Whether you are a developer, IT professional, student, or a curious enthusiast, understanding the cloud's fundamentals is no longer optional—it's essential.

This book, **"Cloud Computing Basics: Understanding AWS, Azure, and Google Cloud,"** is designed to demystify cloud computing. With a focus on real-world applications, it provides a jargon-free, approachable guide to the core concepts and tools that power the cloud. You'll gain not just theoretical knowledge but also practical skills, ensuring you can confidently deploy, manage, and innovate using cloud technologies.

Why This Book?

The cloud computing landscape is vast and constantly evolving, with major players like AWS, Azure, and Google Cloud leading the charge. While each platform offers unique features and tools, their underlying principles and architectures share common foundations. This book bridges the gap, giving you a strong grasp of the basics while delving into the specifics of these three leading platforms.

Most importantly, the book is written with you in mind. Whether you're just starting out or have some experience but feel overwhelmed by the complexity of the cloud, this guide simplifies what can often feel like an intimidating subject. Here's what makes this book different:

1. **Jargon-Free** **Learning**: Technical terms are explained in plain English, ensuring concepts are accessible to everyone, regardless of your background.

2. **Real-World** **Examples**: Each chapter integrates practical scenarios and use cases, showing how businesses leverage cloud services to solve real problems.

3. **Hands-On** **Approach**: Step-by-step guides and walkthroughs provide practical experience with AWS, Azure, and Google Cloud, helping you build confidence and competence.

4. **Balanced** **Coverage**: By covering all three major cloud platforms, this book ensures you have a well-rounded understanding of the

market leaders, enabling you to make informed decisions and comparisons.

Who Is This Book For?

1. **Developers**:
   Gain a solid understanding of cloud services to build, deploy, and scale applications with confidence.
2. **IT** **Professionals**:
   Learn how to migrate infrastructure to the cloud, manage hybrid environments, and optimize costs.
3. **Students** **and** **Enthusiasts**:
   Get introduced to cloud computing fundamentals and prepare for a career in a rapidly growing field.
4. **Business** **Decision-Makers**:
   Understand how cloud computing can transform operations, improve scalability, and reduce costs.

What You'll Learn

This book is structured to take you on a journey from understanding the basics of cloud computing to confidently applying its concepts across platforms. Here's a glimpse of what's covered:

1. **The Fundamentals of Cloud Computing**: Explore what the cloud is, its history, and why it's become the cornerstone of modern IT.

2. **Cloud Computing Models and Concepts**: Learn about the differences between IaaS, PaaS, and SaaS models, and key concepts like virtualization, elasticity, and scalability.

3. **Introduction to Major Cloud Platforms**: Dive into AWS, Azure, and Google Cloud, understanding their core services, strengths, and ideal use cases.

4. **Storage, Compute, and Networking Basics**: Understand how cloud providers handle data storage, server infrastructure, and network connectivity.

5. **Serverless Computing and AI/ML in the Cloud**: Discover how cloud services enable cutting-edge applications, from serverless architectures to AI and machine learning.

6. **Big Data and Analytics**: See how the cloud transforms data processing and analysis, enabling businesses to make smarter decisions.

7. **Cloud Security and Cost Management**: Master best practices for securing cloud environments and managing costs effectively.

8. **Real-World Case Studies**: Examine how industries like healthcare, finance, and education adopt cloud technologies to innovate and excel.

9. **Preparing for the Future**: Explore emerging trends like edge computing, quantum computing, and sustainable cloud practices, and learn how to stay ahead in a rapidly evolving field.

Why Focus on AWS, Azure, and Google Cloud?

While there are many players in the cloud computing space, AWS, Azure, and Google Cloud dominate the market. Together, these three platforms power the majority of the world's cloud-based applications. Each platform has its unique strengths:

- **AWS**: Known for its extensive service offerings and global infrastructure, AWS is the go-to choice for startups, enterprises, and developers.
- **Azure**: With seamless integration into Microsoft's ecosystem, Azure is the top choice for businesses already using Microsoft tools like Windows Server, Active Directory, and Office 365.
- **Google Cloud**: As a leader in data analytics and AI/ML, Google Cloud is the platform of choice for data-driven applications and cutting-edge technologies.

By learning about these platforms, you'll be equipped with the skills to work in virtually any cloud environment.

How to Use This Book

Each chapter builds on the previous one, but the book is designed to be flexible. If you're completely new to the cloud, start from the beginning to build a strong foundation. If you're familiar with the basics, you can dive into specific chapters based on your interests or needs. Real-world examples and hands-on exercises are included throughout to solidify your understanding.

For those interested in certification, this book can also serve as a stepping stone for AWS, Azure, and Google Cloud certification exams by providing foundational knowledge and practical insights.

The Cloud Is the Future—Let's Get Started

As we move into an increasingly digital and interconnected world, cloud computing will continue to play a central role in shaping technology and business. Whether it's enabling remote work, powering AI-driven applications, or supporting global enterprises, the cloud offers endless possibilities.

This book is your gateway to mastering the basics and beginning your journey in the cloud. By the time you finish, you'll not only understand cloud computing but also be ready to apply it in real-world scenarios, opening doors to new opportunities and innovations.

So let's dive in and explore the fascinating world of cloud computing!

CHAPTER 1: INTRODUCTION TO CLOUD COMPUTING

Cloud computing has revolutionized the way businesses and individuals use technology. From hosting websites to running complex machine learning algorithms, cloud platforms have become indispensable for modern innovation. This chapter lays the foundation for understanding cloud computing, tracing its evolution, exploring its benefits and challenges, and examining the major cloud models and leading platforms—AWS, Azure, and Google Cloud.

1.1 Definition and Evolution of Cloud Computing

What Is Cloud Computing?

Cloud computing is the delivery of computing services—such as servers, storage, databases, networking, software, and analytics—over the internet, or "the cloud." Instead of owning physical hardware or managing on-premise infrastructure, users can access resources on-demand, paying only for what they use.

Key Characteristics of Cloud Computing:

- **On-Demand Self-Service**: Users can provision resources like servers and storage without human intervention.
- **Scalability**: Resources can scale up or down based on demand.
- **Pay-as-You-Go Pricing**: Users only pay for the resources they consume.
- **Global Accessibility**: Cloud services are accessible from anywhere with an internet connection.

The Evolution of Cloud Computing: The concept of shared computing resources dates back to the 1960s when John McCarthy, a computer scientist, envisioned the idea of "computing as a utility." Key milestones in cloud computing's evolution include:

1. **1960s: Time-Sharing**
   - Early computers were expensive, so time-sharing allowed multiple users to share a single machine's resources.
2. **1990s: Virtualization and SaaS**

- o The rise of virtualization enabled multiple virtual machines to run on a single physical server.
- o Companies like Salesforce pioneered the Software as a Service (SaaS) model, offering CRM software over the internet.

3. **2006: Launch of AWS**

- o Amazon Web Services (AWS) introduced Elastic Compute Cloud (EC2), marking the beginning of modern cloud computing.

4. **2010s: Growth of Competitors**

- o Microsoft launched Azure (2010), followed by Google Cloud Platform (2011). These platforms introduced diverse services, ranging from data analytics to artificial intelligence.

5. **2020s: The Multi-Cloud Era**

- o Businesses increasingly adopt hybrid and multi-cloud strategies, leveraging multiple providers for flexibility and redundancy.

1.2 Benefits and Challenges of Cloud Adoption

Benefits of Cloud Computing:

1. **Cost Savings**:
    o   Eliminates the need for expensive hardware and on-premise infrastructure.
    o   Pay-as-you-go pricing ensures cost efficiency for varying workloads.

2. **Scalability**:
    o   Easily handle fluctuations in demand by scaling resources up or down.
    o   Ideal for startups and enterprises with unpredictable traffic.

3. **Global Reach**:
    o   Cloud providers have data centers worldwide, enabling low-latency access for global users.

4. **Disaster Recovery**:
    o   Built-in redundancy and automated backups ensure data resilience.

5. **Innovation and Speed**:
    o   Rapidly prototype and deploy applications using ready-made tools like serverless computing and machine learning APIs.

Challenges of Cloud Adoption:

1. **Security Concerns**:

- o Sensitive data stored in the cloud may be vulnerable to breaches.
- o Compliance with regulations like GDPR and HIPAA adds complexity.

2. **Cost Management**:
   - o Uncontrolled resource provisioning can lead to unexpected expenses.

3. **Dependency on Internet Connectivity**:
   - o Downtime or poor connectivity can disrupt operations.

4. **Vendor Lock-In**:
   - o Migrating between providers can be complex and costly due to proprietary services.

5. **Complexity of Management**:
   - o Managing hybrid or multi-cloud environments requires specialized skills.

1.3 Overview of Public, Private, and Hybrid Cloud Models

Cloud computing is not a one-size-fits-all solution. Organizations can choose from three primary models based on their needs.

1. Public Cloud

- Hosted and managed by third-party providers like AWS, Azure, and Google Cloud.
- Resources are shared among multiple users, offering cost efficiency and scalability.

Examples:

- A startup hosting its website on AWS.
- A business analyzing customer data using Google BigQuery.

Advantages:

- Low initial cost.
- Access to a wide range of services.
- Global infrastructure.

Disadvantages:

- Less control over data and infrastructure.
- Potential security concerns.

2. Private Cloud

- Dedicated infrastructure exclusively for one organization, hosted either on-premise or in a private data center.
- Offers greater control and security.

Examples:

- A bank running sensitive financial applications on a private cloud.
- A healthcare provider storing patient records in a private environment.

Advantages:

- Enhanced security and compliance.
- Full control over infrastructure.

Disadvantages:

- High initial setup cost.
- Limited scalability compared to public clouds.

3. Hybrid Cloud

- Combines public and private clouds, allowing organizations to use both for different workloads.
- Ideal for businesses with diverse needs, such as running critical applications privately while leveraging public clouds for analytics.

Examples:

- A retailer storing customer data in a private cloud while running sales analytics on Azure.
- A manufacturing company using Google Cloud for AI-driven supply chain insights and a private cloud for ERP systems.

Advantages:

- Flexibility to choose the best environment for each workload.
- Improved cost management by balancing private and public resources.

Disadvantages:

- Complexity in management and integration.
- Requires expertise to maintain seamless operations.

1.4 Introduction to AWS, Azure, and Google Cloud

AWS, Azure, and Google Cloud collectively dominate the cloud market, each offering a robust suite of services. Let's explore why they have become industry leaders.

Amazon Web Services (AWS):

- **Launched**: 2006
- **Market Share**: Largest share of the cloud market (33% as of 2024).
- **Strengths**:
  - Broadest range of services, from compute (EC2) to machine learning (SageMaker).
  - Mature ecosystem with global data centers.
  - Strong adoption in startups and enterprises.
- **Use Case**: Netflix uses AWS to deliver its video streaming service globally.

Microsoft Azure:

- **Launched**: 2010
- **Market Share**: Second largest (22% as of 2024).
- **Strengths**:
  - Seamless integration with Microsoft products like Office 365 and Windows Server.
  - Popular in enterprise settings.
  - Focus on hybrid cloud with tools like Azure Arc.
- **Use Case**: Johnson Controls uses Azure for IoT solutions in smart buildings.

Google Cloud Platform (GCP):

- **Launched**: 2011
- **Market Share**: Third largest (10% as of 2024).
- **Strengths**:
  - Leadership in AI/ML with tools like TensorFlow and Vertex AI.
  - Competitive pricing for data storage and analytics.
  - Environmentally sustainable infrastructure.
- **Use Case**: Spotify uses GCP for its recommendation engine and analytics.

Why These Platforms Dominate:

1. **Global Infrastructure**:
   - Each provider has data centers worldwide, ensuring low latency and high availability.
2. **Innovation**:
   - Continuous investment in new services, such as AI/ML, serverless computing, and big data analytics.
3. **Ecosystem**:
   - A broad range of services enables businesses to consolidate their needs with one provider.
4. **Trust and Reliability**:

o   Proven track records with enterprises and startups alike.

This chapter introduced the foundational concepts of cloud computing, from its definition and evolution to the benefits and challenges of adoption. We explored the different cloud deployment models—public, private, and hybrid—and examined why AWS, Azure, and Google Cloud dominate the market. As we move into the next chapter, we'll dive deeper into the various cloud service models (IaaS, PaaS, and SaaS) and how they apply to real-world scenarios.

CHAPTER 2: CLOUD COMPUTING MODELS

Cloud computing offers a variety of services tailored to meet the diverse needs of businesses and individuals. These services are generally categorized into three primary models: Infrastructure as a Service (IaaS), Platform as a Service (PaaS), and Software as a Service (SaaS). Each model provides a unique layer of abstraction and functionality, enabling users to focus on specific aspects of their applications and workloads. In this chapter, we'll explore these models, their real-world applications, and their differences across the leading platforms—AWS, Azure, and Google Cloud.

2.1 Explanation of IaaS, PaaS, and SaaS

1. Infrastructure as a Service (IaaS)

Definition:

IaaS provides virtualized computing resources over the internet, such as virtual machines (VMs), storage, and networks. Users control the operating system, applications, and middleware while the cloud provider manages the underlying hardware.

Key Features:

- On-demand provisioning of resources.
- High scalability to accommodate dynamic workloads.
- Pay-as-you-go pricing for cost efficiency.

Use Cases:

- Hosting websites and applications.
- Running development and testing environments.
- Performing data backup and disaster recovery.

2. Platform as a Service (PaaS)

Definition:

PaaS delivers a framework for developers to build, test, and deploy applications without managing the underlying infrastructure. It includes runtime environments, middleware, and development tools.

Key Features:

- Simplifies application development with pre-configured environments.
- Supports multi-language and multi-framework development.
- Often includes tools for CI/CD, database management, and analytics.

Use Cases:

- Rapid application development.
- Automating DevOps pipelines.
- Deploying serverless and containerized applications.

3. Software as a Service (SaaS)

Definition:

SaaS provides fully managed software applications delivered over the internet. Users access applications through web browsers or APIs without worrying about the underlying infrastructure or platform.

Key Features:

- Subscription-based pricing.
- Accessible from anywhere with an internet connection.
- Regular updates and maintenance handled by the provider.

Use Cases:

- Productivity tools like email, collaboration, and CRM.
- E-commerce platforms and customer support applications.
- Analytics and business intelligence tools.

2.2 Real-World Examples of Each Model

Infrastructure as a Service (IaaS)

1. AWS: Amazon EC2

- **Example**: A video streaming startup uses Amazon EC2 to launch virtual machines that handle transcoding and streaming content to users. By dynamically scaling EC2 instances, the startup manages traffic spikes during peak hours.

2. Azure: Virtual Machines

- **Example**: A software company sets up Azure VMs to host legacy applications that are difficult to migrate to modern platforms.

3. Google Cloud: Compute Engine

- **Example**: A gaming company uses Compute Engine to run high-performance servers that power multiplayer gaming sessions.

Platform as a Service (PaaS)

1. AWS: Elastic Beanstalk

- **Example**: A retail company uses Elastic Beanstalk to deploy its online store. The service automatically provisions resources and manages scaling, allowing the company to focus on improving user experience.

2. Azure: App Service

- **Example**: A health-tech startup leverages Azure App Service to build a secure telemedicine platform with minimal effort on infrastructure configuration.

3. Google Cloud: App Engine

- **Example**: An education platform uses App Engine to build and deploy a learning management system with real-time analytics.

Software as a Service (SaaS)

1. AWS: WorkDocs

- **Example**: A law firm uses AWS WorkDocs to collaborate on legal documents securely across different offices.

2. Azure: Office 365

- **Example**: A multinational corporation uses Office 365 for email, document editing, and team collaboration.

3. Google Cloud: Google Workspace

- **Example**: A startup relies on Google Workspace for communication (Gmail), file sharing (Drive), and virtual meetings (Google Meet).

2.3 Differences in Implementation Across AWS, Azure, and Google Cloud

1. Infrastructure as a Service (IaaS)
AWS (Amazon EC2):

- Provides the broadest range of instance types, including general-purpose, compute-optimized, and memory-optimized instances.
- Offers features like Spot Instances for cost savings and Elastic Load Balancing for distributing traffic.

Azure (Virtual Machines):

- Deep integration with Microsoft tools like Active Directory and Windows Server.
- Focuses on hybrid cloud deployments, enabling seamless interaction between on-premise and cloud resources.

Google Cloud (Compute Engine):

- Known for its custom machine types, allowing users to configure CPU and memory precisely.
- Offers preemptible VMs for short-term, cost-efficient workloads.

2. Platform as a Service (PaaS)

AWS (Elastic Beanstalk):

- Simplifies application deployment for web and mobile apps.
- Supports multiple programming languages, including Python, Java, Node.js, and Ruby.

Azure (App Service):

- Strong focus on enterprise applications with built-in security and compliance features.
- Provides integration with Azure DevOps for CI/CD pipelines.

Google Cloud (App Engine):

- Offers both standard and flexible environments, allowing developers to balance simplicity with customizability.
- Includes automatic scaling based on request volume.

33

3. Software as a Service (SaaS)

AWS:

- SaaS offerings are focused on enterprise productivity, such as WorkSpaces (virtual desktops) and WorkDocs.

Azure:

- Strong presence in enterprise SaaS with tools like Office 365, Dynamics 365 (CRM/ERP), and Power BI.

Google Cloud:

- Popular for consumer and business SaaS tools like Gmail, Google Drive, and Google Meet.

Comparison Table of IaaS, PaaS, and SaaS

Aspect	IaaS	PaaS	SaaS
Control Level	High (OS and applications)	Medium (application only)	Low (pre-built software)
Target Audience	System administrators, IT teams	Developers	End-users

Aspect	IaaS	PaaS	SaaS
Examples	AWS EC2, Azure VMs, GCE	AWS Beanstalk, Azure App Service, GAE	Office 365, Google Workspace
Customization	High	Moderate	Minimal
Management Responsibility	User manages most components	Provider manages the platform	Provider manages everything

Understanding the cloud computing models—Infrastructure as a Service (IaaS), Platform as a Service (PaaS), and Software as a Service (SaaS)—is essential for leveraging the cloud effectively. Each model serves distinct purposes and offers unique benefits, allowing businesses to choose the best fit for their requirements. As we progress through this book, you'll see how these models are applied in real-world scenarios, and how AWS, Azure, and Google Cloud implement them to empower businesses and developers alike. In the next chapter, we'll explore foundational concepts like virtualization, containers, and serverless computing that underpin modern cloud services.

CHAPTER 3: KEY CONCEPTS IN CLOUD COMPUTING

Cloud computing is built on a foundation of innovative concepts and technologies that enable flexibility, efficiency, and resilience. Understanding these key concepts—virtualization, containers, serverless computing, elasticity, scalability, and high availability—is critical to leveraging the full potential of the cloud. This chapter explains these technologies and principles with real-world examples, including how e-commerce platforms scale during peak seasons.

3.1 Virtualization, Containers, and Serverless Computing

1. Virtualization

Definition:

Virtualization is the process of creating virtual versions of computing resources, such as servers, storage, and networks. A single physical machine can run multiple virtual machines (VMs), each with its own operating system and applications.

How It Works:

- Virtualization relies on a **hypervisor**, a layer of software that manages the virtual machines and allocates physical resources like CPU, memory, and storage.

Benefits:

- **Resource Utilization**: Maximizes hardware efficiency by running multiple VMs on a single server.
- **Cost Savings**: Reduces the need for physical servers.
- **Flexibility**: Allows easy provisioning and scaling of VMs.

Real-World Example:

- A small business runs multiple applications (e.g., a CRM system, web server, and database) on separate VMs, all hosted on a single physical server, minimizing costs while maintaining isolation between applications.

2. Containers

Definition:

Containers are lightweight, portable units of software that package an application and its dependencies together. Unlike virtual machines, containers share the host operating system but remain isolated from one another.

Key Tools:

- **Docker**: The most popular containerization platform.
- **Kubernetes**: A container orchestration tool for managing containerized applications at scale.

Benefits:

- **Portability**: Containers can run consistently across environments (development, testing, production).
- **Efficiency**: Use fewer resources than VMs because they don't require a full operating system.
- **Scalability**: Containers are faster to start and stop, making them ideal for dynamic workloads.

Real-World Example:

- A development team uses Docker containers to build, test, and deploy microservices, ensuring that the application behaves the same across local machines and production servers.

3. Serverless Computing

Definition:

Serverless computing allows developers to build and run applications without managing servers. The cloud provider handles all infrastructure, automatically scaling resources based on demand.

How It Works:

- Developers write code as small functions, which are triggered by specific events (e.g., HTTP requests, database changes).
- The cloud provider executes the functions and charges based on the number of executions and runtime.

Benefits:

- **Cost Efficiency**: Pay only for the compute time consumed, not idle resources.
- **Simplified Operations**: No need to manage servers, enabling developers to focus on code.

Examples:

- **AWS Lambda**: Executes functions in response to events.
- **Azure Functions**: Integrates with Azure services for event-driven workflows.

- **Google Cloud Functions**: Scales automatically based on incoming requests.

Real-World Example:

- An e-commerce platform uses AWS Lambda to send email notifications when an order is placed, ensuring scalability during high-traffic periods like Black Friday.

3.2 Elasticity, Scalability, and High Availability

1. Elasticity
Definition:
Elasticity refers to the ability to automatically scale resources up or down based on demand, ensuring optimal resource utilization.

Example:

- A news website experiences a surge in traffic during breaking news events. Elastic load balancers and auto-scaling groups provision additional servers to handle the traffic spike, then scale back down during off-peak hours.

2. Scalability

Definition:

Scalability is the ability of a system to handle increased workload by adding resources (scaling up or scaling out).

Types of Scalability:

1. **Vertical Scaling (Scale-Up)**:
   - Increases the capacity of a single server (e.g., adding more CPU or RAM).
   - Example: Upgrading an AWS EC2 instance type from t2.micro to t2.large.
2. **Horizontal Scaling (Scale-Out)**:
   - Adds more servers or instances to distribute the load.
   - Example: Adding multiple Azure Virtual Machines behind a load balancer.

Real-World Example:

- A social media platform adds servers during a major global event to ensure seamless user experience despite millions of concurrent logins.

3. High Availability
Definition:

High availability ensures that a system is operational and accessible even during failures, achieved through redundancy and failover mechanisms.

Techniques for High Availability:

- **Replication**: Duplicating data across multiple servers or regions.
- **Load Balancing**: Distributing traffic across multiple servers to prevent overload.
- **Failover**: Automatically switching to a backup system in case of failure.

Real-World Example:

- A financial institution uses Google Cloud Spanner for a globally distributed, highly available database system that guarantees uptime for critical applications.

3.3 Real-World Use Case: E-Commerce Scalability During Peak Seasons

Scenario:

An e-commerce company prepares for Black Friday, expecting a 10x increase in traffic. It must ensure smooth customer experiences, including fast website performance, real-time inventory updates, and secure payment processing.

Solution Using Cloud Computing:

1. Virtualization for Flexibility:

- The company uses AWS EC2 instances to host its web servers, enabling quick provisioning of additional VMs during peak traffic.

2. Containers for Microservices:

- The application is containerized using Docker, with services like catalog management, inventory tracking, and payment processing running in Kubernetes clusters.

3. Serverless Functions for Scalability:

- AWS Lambda processes real-time order placements, scaling automatically as traffic spikes.

4. Elastic Load Balancers for Distribution:

- An Elastic Load Balancer ensures that incoming requests are evenly distributed across multiple EC2 instances, preventing any single server from being overwhelmed.

5. High Availability for Redundancy:

- The database is replicated across multiple regions using AWS RDS Multi-AZ Deployment, ensuring uptime even if one region experiences an outage.

6. Real-Time Monitoring:

- AWS CloudWatch monitors server health, traffic patterns, and application performance, triggering alerts for potential issues.

Outcome:

- The e-commerce platform handles millions of transactions without downtime, ensuring customer satisfaction and maximizing sales.

This chapter introduced foundational technologies like virtualization, containers, and serverless computing that underpin cloud computing. It also explained key principles such as elasticity, scalability, and high availability, which ensure that cloud systems can adapt to changing demands while maintaining performance and reliability. Real-world use cases, like e-commerce scalability during peak seasons, demonstrate how these concepts come to life in practical applications. In the next chapter, we'll explore how to get started with AWS, Azure, and Google Cloud, setting up your first accounts and navigating their interfaces.

CHAPTER 4: GETTING STARTED WITH AWS

Amazon Web Services (AWS) is one of the most widely used cloud computing platforms in the world. It offers a vast array of services that cater to compute, storage, networking, machine learning, analytics, and much more. This chapter will guide you through the foundational steps of working with AWS, including setting up your account, navigating the AWS Management Console, and deploying your first web application.

4.1 Overview of AWS Services and Console

AWS provides over 200 fully featured services for a wide range of applications. Here's a quick overview of its most essential services:

1. Compute Services

- **Amazon EC2 (Elastic Compute Cloud)**:
  - o Virtual servers for hosting applications.
  - o Flexible instance types for diverse workloads.
- **AWS Lambda**:
  - o Serverless compute service that runs your code in response to events.
- **Elastic Beanstalk**:
  - o Simplified deployment and scaling of web applications.

2. Storage Services

- **Amazon S3 (Simple Storage Service)**:
  - o Object storage for data like images, videos, and backups.
- **EBS (Elastic Block Store)**:
  - o Persistent storage for EC2 instances.
- **Glacier**:
  - o Low-cost archival storage.

3. Networking Services

- **VPC (Virtual Private Cloud)**:
  - o Isolated networks within AWS for secure resources.
- **Route 53**:
  - o Domain name system (DNS) for routing traffic to AWS resources.

- **Elastic Load Balancer (ELB)**:
  - o Distributes incoming traffic across multiple servers.

4. Database Services

- **Amazon RDS (Relational Database Service)**:
  - o Managed databases for SQL workloads.
- **DynamoDB**:
  - o Fully managed NoSQL database.
- **Redshift**:
  - o Data warehouse for big data analytics.

5. Monitoring and Management

- **AWS CloudWatch**:
  - o Monitoring logs, metrics, and events.
- **CloudFormation**:
  - o Infrastructure as code for resource provisioning.
- **AWS IAM (Identity and Access Management)**:
  - o Manage user access and permissions.

AWS Management Console: The AWS Management Console is a web-based interface where you can access and manage AWS services. It is organized into:

- **Services menu**: Lists all available AWS services.
- **Search bar**: Quickly locate specific services.

- **Resource groups**: View and manage resources grouped by tags or applications.

4.2 Setting Up Your First AWS Account

To start using AWS, you need to create an account. Follow these steps:

Step 1: Create an AWS Account

1. Visit the <u>AWS sign-up page</u>.
2. Click **Create an AWS Account**.
3. Enter your email address, choose a password, and specify your account name.
4. Provide your billing information (a credit card is required).
5. Verify your identity using a phone number or SMS.
6. Select a support plan (choose the **Free Tier** for learning purposes).

Step 2: Activate Free Tier Services

AWS Free Tier provides limited usage of many services at no cost, including:

- 750 hours of EC2 t2.micro instances per month.
- 5 GB of Amazon S3 storage.
- 1 million free Lambda requests per month.

Step 3: Secure Your Account

- Enable **Multi-Factor Authentication (MFA)** for added security:

    1. Navigate to **My Security Credentials**.
    2. Select **Activate MFA** and follow the steps to set up an authenticator app.

4.3 Navigating the AWS Management Console

Once your account is set up, the AWS Management Console becomes your main interface for interacting with AWS services. Here's how to navigate it:

1. Dashboard

- The homepage shows shortcuts to commonly used services, recent activity, and helpful resources.

2. Service Categories

- The services menu is categorized by function (e.g., Compute, Storage, Databases).
- You can also pin frequently used services for quick access.

3. Account Management

- Access account settings, billing details, and IAM settings from the top-right menu.

4. Launching Services

- Use the search bar to locate a service (e.g., EC2) and click to launch its dashboard.

5. Regions

- AWS services are hosted in multiple geographic regions.
- Select the region closest to your users for better performance.

4.4 Real-World Example: Deploying a Simple Web Application on AWS

Scenario:

You are building a simple web application to display a static portfolio site using AWS services. The application will be hosted on an EC2 instance.

Steps to Deploy:

Step 1: Launch an EC2 Instance

1. Navigate to the AWS Management Console.
2. Search for **EC2** in the services menu and click **Launch Instance**.
3. Choose an Amazon Machine Image (AMI):
   o Select **Amazon Linux 2 AMI (Free Tier eligible)**.
4. Select an instance type:

  o Choose **t2.micro (Free Tier eligible).**

5. Configure instance details:

  o Accept defaults and proceed.

6. Add storage:

  o Use the default storage size (8 GB).

7. Add tags:

  o Tag your instance (e.g., Name = MyWebApp).

8. Configure a security group:

  o Add rules to allow HTTP (port 80) and SSH (port 22) traffic.

9. Launch the instance:

  o Download the private key file (e.g., my-key.pem) for SSH access.

Step 2: Connect to Your Instance

1. Open a terminal or SSH client.

2. Use the following command to connect:

bash

ssh -i my-key.pem ec2-user@<your-ec2-public-ip>

Step 3: Install and Configure a Web Server

1. Update the package manager:

bash

```
sudo yum update -y
```

2. Install Apache:

bash

```
sudo yum install httpd -y
```

3. Start the Apache server:

bash

```
sudo systemctl start httpd
sudo systemctl enable httpd
```

4. Create a simple HTML file:

bash

```
echo "<h1>Welcome to My Web App</h1>" | sudo tee
/var/www/html/index.html
```

Step 4: Access Your Web Application

- Open a web browser and navigate to your EC2 instance's public IP address.

- You should see your web application displaying the message: **"Welcome to My Web App"**.

Step 5: Monitor and Scale

- Use **AWS CloudWatch** to monitor the performance of your EC2 instance.
- Configure auto-scaling if traffic increases significantly.

This chapter provided a hands-on introduction to AWS, starting with an overview of its services and guiding you through account setup and console navigation. By deploying a simple web application, you've gained practical experience with key AWS tools like EC2 and learned how to create a secure and scalable environment. In the next chapter, we'll explore Azure, diving into its unique offerings and setting up a basic Azure account.

CHAPTER 5: GETTING STARTED WITH AZURE

Microsoft Azure is a leading cloud platform that provides an extensive range of cloud services for compute, storage, databases, AI, and more. With its strong focus on hybrid cloud solutions and integration with Microsoft's ecosystem, Azure is a top choice for enterprises and developers alike. In this chapter, we'll explore Azure's services, guide you through setting up an account, navigating the Azure portal, and deploying your first virtual machine.

5.1 Overview of Azure Services and Portal

Azure offers over 200 services, designed to meet diverse application and infrastructure needs. Here's a snapshot of its core offerings:

1. Compute Services

- **Azure Virtual Machines**:
  - o Fully customizable virtual servers for running applications.
- **Azure App Service**:
  - o A managed platform for deploying web apps and APIs.
- **Azure Functions**:
  - o Serverless compute service for event-driven workloads.

2. Storage Services

- **Blob Storage**:
  - o Object storage for unstructured data like videos and backups.
- **Azure Files**:
  - o Fully managed file shares in the cloud.
- **Disk Storage**:
  - o High-performance block storage for Azure VMs.

3. Networking Services

- **Virtual Network (VNet)**:
  - o Isolated networks for secure resource communication.

- **Azure Load Balancer**:
  - o Distributes traffic across multiple resources for high availability.
- **Azure Front Door**:
  - o Provides global load balancing and content delivery.

4. Database Services

- **Azure SQL Database**:
  - o Fully managed relational database with automatic updates and scaling.
- **Cosmos DB**:
  - o A globally distributed, multi-model NoSQL database.
- **Azure Database for PostgreSQL**:
  - o Managed PostgreSQL with high availability and scaling.

5. Monitoring and Management

- **Azure Monitor**:
  - o Comprehensive monitoring of applications and infrastructure.
- **Azure Resource Manager (ARM)**:
  - o Manages resources as declarative code.
- **Azure Security Center**:
  - o Protects against threats and ensures compliance.

Azure   **Portal**:

The Azure Portal is a web-based interface for accessing and managing all Azure services. It offers:

- **Dashboards**: Customizable views for resource monitoring.
- **Resource Groups**: Logical containers for managing related resources.
- **Integrated Tools**: Direct access to monitoring, billing, and analytics.

5.2 Setting Up Your First Azure Account

Step 1: Create an Azure Account

1. Visit the Azure sign-up page.
2. Click **Start Free** to create an account.
3. Provide your personal or business email address and set up a Microsoft account.
4. Verify your identity by providing a phone number and credit card details.
   - You'll receive **$200 in free credits** to explore Azure services.

Step 2: Activate Free Tier Services

Azure's Free Tier includes:

- 750 hours of Linux or Windows virtual machines.

- 5 GB of Blob Storage.
- 250 GB of SQL Database storage.
- Access to AI and machine learning tools like Cognitive Services.

Step 3: Secure Your Account

- Enable **Multi-Factor Authentication (MFA)** for additional security.
    1. Navigate to **Azure Active Directory** in the portal.
    2. Set up MFA using an authenticator app or SMS.

5.3 Exploring the Azure Portal and Dashboard

The Azure Portal is your command center for managing Azure services. Let's explore its key components:

1. Dashboard

- The default home screen provides an overview of your resources and services.
- Customize the dashboard by pinning frequently used resources, like virtual machines or storage accounts.

2. Navigation Menu

- Access all Azure services through the left-hand menu.

- Use the search bar to locate specific resources or tools quickly.

3. Resource Management

- Resources are grouped into **Resource Groups** for better organization.
- Resource groups simplify deployment, management, and billing.

4. Monitoring and Alerts

- **Azure Monitor** tracks performance metrics, logs, and alerts for all resources.
- Set up custom alerts for events like high CPU usage or resource failures.

5. Regions

- Azure operates in **60+ global regions**.
- Select the region closest to your users to minimize latency.

5.4 Real-World Example: Deploying a Virtual Machine on Azure

Scenario:

You want to deploy a virtual machine (VM) to host a web application for testing purposes.

Steps to Deploy:

Step 1: Create a Resource Group

1. Navigate to **Resource Groups** in the Azure Portal.
2. Click **+ Create** and enter:
   - **Name**: WebAppResourceGroup
   - **Region**: Choose a location close to your users.
3. Click **Review + Create** to finalize.

Step 2: Launch a Virtual Machine

1. Search for **Virtual Machines** in the portal and click **+ Create**.
2. Select **Azure Virtual Machine** from the options.
3. Configure the VM:
   - **Name**: MyWebAppVM
   - **Region**: Same as the resource group.
   - **Image**: Choose **Ubuntu Server 20.04 LTS**.
   - **Size**: Select **Standard B1s (Free Tier eligible)**.
   - **Authentication**: Use an SSH key or password for secure access.
4. Click **Review + Create** and then **Create**.

Step 3: Connect to Your VM

1. Navigate to the VM in the portal.

2. Copy the **Public IP Address**.

3. Open a terminal or SSH client and connect:

bash

ssh azureuser@<public-ip-address>

Step 4: Install a Web Server

1. Update the package manager:

bash

sudo apt update

2. Install Apache:

bash

sudo apt install apache2 -y

3. Start the Apache server:

bash

sudo systemctl start apache2

4. Confirm that the web server is running:

bash

sudo systemctl status apache2

Step 5: Access Your Web Application

- Open a web browser and navigate to your VM's public IP address.
- You should see the Apache default welcome page.

Step 6: Monitor Your VM

- Use **Azure Monitor** to track CPU, memory, and disk usage.
- Set up alerts for abnormal performance to ensure uptime.

In this chapter, we explored the essentials of getting started with Azure, from understanding its services to setting up your first account. The Azure Portal serves as a powerful tool for managing resources, and deploying a virtual machine provides hands-on experience with its capabilities. By learning to use Azure effectively, you can harness its potential for building scalable, secure, and reliable applications. In the next chapter, we'll dive into Google Cloud, exploring its unique features and deploying a basic application.

CHAPTER 6: GETTING STARTED WITH GOOGLE CLOUD

Google Cloud Platform (GCP) is a robust cloud computing service offering from Google, known for its cutting-edge technology, competitive pricing, and leadership in AI/ML capabilities. With services ranging from compute and storage to big data and machine learning, GCP is a favorite among businesses seeking innovation and scalability. This chapter introduces GCP's core services, guides you through setting up an account, navigating the Google Cloud Console, and deploying a static website.

6.1 Overview of Google Cloud Services and Console

Google Cloud offers over 100 services to address diverse needs in computing, storage, networking, data analytics, AI/ML, and more. Below is an overview of its key offerings:

1. Compute Services

- **Compute Engine**:
  - Virtual machines for flexible and scalable compute resources.
- **Google Kubernetes Engine (GKE)**:
  - Managed Kubernetes for containerized applications.
- **App Engine**:
  - Fully managed PaaS for deploying web applications.
- **Cloud Functions**:
  - Serverless functions for event-driven applications.

2. Storage Services

- **Cloud Storage**:
  - Object storage for unstructured data like images and backups.
- **Persistent Disk**:
  - Block storage for Compute Engine and GKE.
- **Filestore**:
  - Fully managed file storage for applications needing shared storage.

3. Networking Services

- **Cloud Load Balancing**:
  - ○ Distributes traffic across multiple backend resources globally.
- **VPC (Virtual Private Cloud)**:
  - ○ Isolated networks for secure resource communication.
- **Cloud CDN**:
  - ○ Delivers content with low latency using Google's global edge network.

4. Database Services

- **Cloud SQL**:
  - ○ Fully managed relational databases like MySQL, PostgreSQL, and SQL Server.
- **BigQuery**:
  - ○ A serverless, highly scalable data warehouse for analytics.
- **Firestore**:
  - ○ A NoSQL database for real-time application data.

5. Machine Learning and AI

- **Vertex AI**:

- o A unified platform for training and deploying machine learning models.
- **Natural Language API**:
    - o Tools for sentiment analysis, entity recognition, and text classification.
- **Vision AI**:
    - o Image recognition and analysis.

Google   Cloud   Console:
The Google Cloud Console is a web-based management interface for all Google Cloud services. It includes tools for provisioning, monitoring, and managing resources, offering both command-line and web-based access.

6.2 Setting Up Your First Google Cloud Account

Step 1: Create a Google Cloud Account

1. Visit the Google Cloud website.
2. Click **Get started for free**.
3. Sign in with your Google account or create a new one.
4. Provide billing information:
    - o You'll receive $300 in free credits for 90 days to explore GCP services.

Step 2: Secure Your Account

- Enable **2-Step Verification** for additional security.
- Configure **IAM** **roles** to control user access and permissions.

Step 3: Activate Free Tier Services

GCP's Free Tier includes:

- 50 GB of standard Cloud Storage.
- 1 f1-micro VM instance per month (in select regions).
- 1 GB of BigQuery storage.

6.3 Introduction to the Google Cloud Console

The Google Cloud Console is the central hub for managing GCP resources. Here's an overview of its key components:

1. Navigation Menu

- Located on the left-hand side, the navigation menu categorizes services by function (e.g., Compute, Storage, Networking).

2. Dashboard

- The default home screen displays a high-level overview of resources, billing, and activity logs.

- Customize the dashboard to monitor specific projects or resources.

3. Resource Management

- Projects are the primary organizational unit in GCP.
- Each project has its own billing, permissions, and resources.

4. Cloud Shell

- A built-in command-line interface accessible directly from the console.
- Pre-configured with tools like gcloud, Python, and Docker.

5. Regions and Zones

- Google Cloud operates in **35+ regions and 100+ zones**.
- Select regions close to your users to optimize performance and reduce latency.

6.4 Real-World Example: Hosting a Static Website on Google Cloud

Scenario:

You want to host a static portfolio website (HTML, CSS, and JavaScript files) on Google Cloud using **Cloud Storage**.

Steps to Host a Static Website:

Step 1: Create a Cloud Storage Bucket

1. In the Google Cloud Console, navigate to **Storage** → **Buckets**.
2. Click + **Create Bucket** and configure:
   - **Bucket Name**: my-portfolio-website.
   - **Location**: Choose a region (e.g., us-central1).
   - **Storage Class**: Select **Standard**.
   - **Access Control**: Choose **Uniform**.

Step 2: Enable Public Access

1. Open the bucket and go to the **Permissions** tab.
2. Click + **Add** and add the following entry:
   - **Principal**: allUsers
   - **Role**: Storage Object Viewer
3. Confirm to make the bucket publicly accessible.

Step 3: Upload Website Files

1. Navigate to your bucket and click **Upload Files**.
2. Upload your static website files (e.g., index.html, styles.css).

Step 4: Configure Website Settings

1. In the bucket settings, go to the **Edit Website Configuration** section.
2. Set:
   - **Main Page**: index.html
   - **Error Page**: 404.html
3. Save the configuration.

Step 5: Access Your Website

- Your website will be accessible at:

bash

http://storage.googleapis.com/<bucket-name>/index.html

Optional Enhancements:

- Use **Cloud CDN** to improve performance by caching content at Google's global edge locations.
- Configure a custom domain with **Cloud DNS** for a professional URL (e.g., www.myportfolio.com).

Real-World Use Case: Static Website for a Small Business

Scenario:

A local bakery wants a simple website to showcase its menu, location, and contact information.

Solution:

1. Design a basic website using HTML and CSS.
2. Host the site on Google Cloud Storage for low-cost, reliable storage.
3. Use **Cloud DNS** to link the website to a custom domain (e.g., www.localbakery.com).

Outcome:

- The bakery's website is live and accessible globally with minimal setup costs, demonstrating the ease and scalability of Google Cloud.

This chapter provided a hands-on introduction to Google Cloud, from setting up an account to navigating the Google Cloud Console. By hosting a static website, you've experienced GCP's simplicity and power for managing web resources. As we move forward, you'll learn about core concepts like cloud storage, compute services, and serverless solutions in greater depth, building on this foundational knowledge. In the next chapter, we'll dive into the essentials of cloud storage, comparing offerings across AWS, Azure, and Google Cloud.

CHAPTER 7: CLOUD STORAGE BASICS

Cloud storage is a fundamental component of modern cloud computing, enabling businesses to store, retrieve, and manage vast amounts of data. Whether it's storing static assets for a website or backing up critical business data, cloud storage services offer flexibility, scalability, and security. In this chapter, we'll explore the core storage offerings from AWS, Azure, and Google Cloud, compare their pricing and performance, and walk through a real-world example of setting up cloud storage for a video streaming service.

7.1 Overview of Storage Services

Each cloud provider offers a comprehensive storage solution tailored to different use cases. Let's dive into the key features and offerings of AWS S3, Azure Blob Storage, and Google Cloud Storage.

1. AWS S3 (Simple Storage Service)

Overview:

AWS S3 is an object storage service that provides highly durable and scalable storage for a variety of use cases, including backups, data lakes, and web hosting.

Key Features:

- **Durability**: 99.999999999% (11 nines) durability ensures data integrity.
- **Storage Classes**:
    - **Standard**: High-performance storage for frequently accessed data.

- o **Intelligent-Tiering**: Automatically moves data to the most cost-effective storage tier.
  - o **Glacier**: Low-cost storage for archival data.
- **S3 Bucket Policies**: Define access permissions at the bucket level.
- **Versioning**: Maintain multiple versions of an object for backup and recovery.

2. Azure Blob Storage

Overview:

Azure Blob Storage is a scalable and secure object storage solution for unstructured data like images, videos, and documents.

Key Features:

- **Storage Tiers**:
  - o **Hot**: Optimized for frequently accessed data.
  - o **Cool**: Designed for infrequently accessed data with lower storage costs.
  - o **Archive**: Ultra-low-cost storage for rarely accessed data.
- **Blob Types**:
  - o **Block Blobs**: Optimized for streaming and storing large amounts of text or binary data.
  - o **Append Blobs**: Ideal for log storage.
  - o **Page Blobs**: Suited for random access workloads.

- **Secure Access**: Offers integration with Azure Active Directory (AAD) for granular permissions.

3. Google Cloud Storage

Overview:

Google Cloud Storage is a unified object storage solution that supports both live data and archival data in the same service.

Key Features:

- **Storage Classes**:
  - **Standard**: High-performance storage for active workloads.
  - **Nearline**: Cost-effective for data accessed less than once a month.
  - **Coldline**: For data accessed less than once a year.
  - **Archive**: Lowest-cost option for long-term storage.
- **Object Lifecycle Management**: Automatically moves objects to different storage classes based on pre-defined rules.
- **Multi-Regional Storage**: Provides global access with high availability.

7.2 Differences in Pricing and Performance

1. Pricing Comparison

Storage Costs (as of 2024; pricing varies by region):

- **AWS S3**:
    - Standard: $0.023/GB per month.
    - Glacier: $0.004/GB per month.
- **Azure Blob Storage**:
    - Hot: $0.018/GB per month.
    - Archive: $0.002/GB per month.
- **Google Cloud Storage**:
    - Standard: $0.020/GB per month.
    - Archive: $0.0012/GB per month.

Data Transfer Costs:

- All providers charge for outbound data transfer (egress) from their networks:
    - AWS: $0.09/GB for the first 10 TB.
    - Azure: $0.087/GB for the first 10 TB.
    - Google Cloud: $0.12/GB for the first 1 TB, with discounts for higher volumes.

2. Performance Comparison

Performance depends on factors like storage class, region, and network speed:

- **AWS S3**: Known for consistent performance and global reach with multi-region support.

- **Azure Blob Storage**: Strong integration with Microsoft services, making it ideal for enterprises using the Microsoft ecosystem.
- **Google Cloud Storage**: High throughput and low-latency access, favored for analytics and AI/ML workloads.

7.3 Real-World Example: Setting Up Cloud Storage for a Video Streaming Service

Scenario:

You're building a video streaming service where users can upload, stream, and download videos. The storage solution must handle large file uploads, serve files with low latency, and scale with increasing user demand.

Steps to Set Up Cloud Storage for Video Streaming

Step 1: Choose a Cloud Storage Provider

- For this example, we'll use **AWS S3**, but the process is similar for Azure Blob Storage and Google Cloud Storage.

Step 2: Create a Storage Bucket

1. In the AWS Management Console, navigate to **S3** and click **Create Bucket**.
2. Configure the bucket:
    o **Name**: video-streaming-bucket.

- o **Region**: Select a region close to your target audience (e.g., us-east-1).
- o **Public Access Settings**: Restrict public access to keep the bucket private.

3. Click **Create Bucket**.

Step 3: Configure Permissions

- Use **IAM Roles** to grant your application access to the bucket:
  1. Go to the **IAM** service and create a role for your application.
  2. Attach the AmazonS3FullAccess policy to the role.

Step 4: Enable Lifecycle Policies

- Configure a lifecycle rule to automatically move older videos to a lower-cost storage class:
  1. Open the bucket and navigate to the **Management** tab.
  2. Click **Create lifecycle rule** and set conditions (e.g., move files to Glacier after 90 days).

Step 5: Integrate with the Application

- Use the AWS SDK (e.g., Boto3 for Python) to upload and retrieve video files.

Example: Uploading a video file.

python

```
import boto3

s3 = boto3.client('s3')
bucket_name = 'video-streaming-bucket'
file_name = 'example_video.mp4'

# Upload the video to S3
s3.upload_file(file_name, bucket_name, file_name)
```

Step 6: Optimize Content Delivery

- Use **Amazon CloudFront** to distribute video content with low latency:
    1. In the AWS Console, go to **CloudFront** and create a new distribution.
    2. Set the S3 bucket as the origin.
    3. Enable caching to improve performance.

Outcome

With AWS S3 and CloudFront:

- Videos are securely stored and served with minimal latency.

- Lifecycle rules ensure cost efficiency as older videos move to Glacier.
- Scalability and durability handle increasing user uploads and streaming demands.

This chapter provided an in-depth understanding of cloud storage services, comparing AWS S3, Azure Blob Storage, and Google Cloud Storage in terms of features, pricing, and performance. By walking through the real-world example of a video streaming service, you've gained practical insights into setting up scalable and cost-effective cloud storage solutions. In the next chapter, we'll explore compute services across cloud platforms, focusing on virtual machines, containerization, and serverless computing.

CHAPTER 8: COMPUTE SERVICES IN THE CLOUD

Compute services are at the core of cloud computing, providing the processing power required to run applications, host websites, and manage workloads. Each cloud provider offers flexible compute services that cater to diverse needs, from virtual machines to containerized and serverless solutions. This chapter explores compute offerings from AWS, Azure, and Google Cloud, compares their features, and walks you through launching and managing a virtual server.

8.1 Understanding EC2, Virtual Machines, and Compute Engine

1. Amazon EC2 (Elastic Compute Cloud)

Overview:

Amazon EC2 is a scalable virtual server solution that allows users to run applications on demand with complete control over the operating system, storage, and networking.

Key Features:

- **Instance Types**: A wide range of instances tailored for compute, memory, or storage optimization.
  - Example: General-purpose (t2, t3), compute-optimized (c5), and GPU-based (p4) instances.
- **Elasticity**: Automatically scale up or down based on workload.
- **Spot Instances**: Cost-effective option for non-critical workloads.
- **Security**: Integrated with AWS Identity and Access Management (IAM) for access control.

Use Cases:

- Hosting web applications.
- Running batch processing jobs.
- Training machine learning models on GPU-enabled instances.

2. *Azure Virtual Machines*

Overview:

Azure Virtual Machines offer scalable and flexible compute resources for running applications in the cloud. These VMs integrate seamlessly with Microsoft's ecosystem.

Key Features:

- **Instance Sizes**: Supports a variety of VM sizes, from general-purpose (B-series) to specialized workloads like GPU (NC-series) and high-performance computing.
- **Hybrid Cloud Integration**: Works seamlessly with on-premises infrastructure using Azure Arc.
- **Auto-Scaling**: Dynamic scaling of VM instances to meet demand.
- **Pre-Configured Images**: Includes a library of OS images like Windows Server and Ubuntu.

Use Cases:

- Migrating on-premises workloads to the cloud.
- Hosting databases and ERP systems.
- Running development and testing environments.

3. *Google Cloud Compute Engine*

Overview:

Compute Engine provides virtual machines running on Google's global infrastructure. It offers flexibility with pre-configured and custom machine types.

Key Features:

- **Custom Machine Types**: Allows users to specify the exact number of CPUs and memory.
- **Sustained-Use Discounts**: Automatically applies discounts for long-running instances.
- **Preemptible VMs**: Low-cost instances ideal for batch jobs.
- **Integrated with Kubernetes**: Runs containerized applications using Kubernetes.

Use Cases:

- High-performance computing.
- Data processing pipelines.
- Hosting containerized applications.

8.2 Comparison of Compute Services Across Platforms

Feature	AWS EC2	Azure Virtual Machines	Google Compute Engine
Customization	Wide range of instance types	Pre-configured and custom sizes	Flexible custom machine types
Pricing Models	On-demand, Reserved, Spot Instances	Pay-as-you-go, Reserved, Spot VMs	Pay-as-you-go, Preemptible VMs
Auto-Scaling	Yes	Yes	Yes
Integration	Best for AWS ecosystem	Seamless with Microsoft products	Strong with AI/ML and Kubernetes
Cost Optimization	Spot Instances for savings	Low priority VMs for cost reduction	Sustained-use and preemptible discounts

8.3 Real-World Example: Launching and Managing a Virtual Server

Scenario:

A startup needs a virtual server to host its web application. The server should be scalable, secure, and cost-effective.

Steps to Launch and Manage a Virtual Server

Step 1: Choose a Cloud Provider

For this example, we'll use **AWS EC2**, but the process is similar for Azure and Google Cloud.

Step 2: Create and Configure a Virtual Server

Launch an EC2 Instance (AWS):

1. Navigate to the AWS Management Console and search for **EC2**.
2. Click **Launch Instance** and follow these steps:
   - **Step 1: Choose AMI**:
     - Select **Amazon Linux 2 AMI (Free Tier eligible)**.
   - **Step 2: Choose Instance Type**:
     - Select **t2.micro (Free Tier eligible)**.
   - **Step 3: Configure Instance**:
     - Accept default settings or specify details like auto-scaling.
   - **Step 4: Add Storage**:
     - Set the default size (e.g., 8 GB).
   - **Step 5: Configure Security Group**:

- Allow inbound HTTP (port 80) and SSH (port 22) traffic.
  - **Step 6: Review and Launch**:
    - Download the private key file (.pem) for SSH access.
    - Click **Launch** to create the instance.

Step 3: Connect to Your Virtual Server

Using SSH:

1. Open a terminal and navigate to the folder containing your .pem file.
2. Connect to your EC2 instance:

bash

ssh -i my-key.pem ec2-user@<public-ip-address>

3. You now have shell access to your virtual server.

Step 4: Install and Configure a Web Server

1. Update the package manager:

bash

```
sudo yum update -y
```

2. Install Apache:

bash

```
sudo yum install httpd -y
```

3. Start the Apache service:

bash

```
sudo systemctl start httpd
sudo systemctl enable httpd
```

4. Create a simple HTML page:

bash

```
echo "<h1>Welcome to My Web Application</h1>" | sudo tee /var/www/html/index.html
```

Step 5: Access the Web Application

1. Open a browser and navigate to your EC2 instance's public IP address.

2. You should see the message: **"Welcome to My Web Application"**.

Step 6: Manage the Server

Monitor Performance:

- Use **AWS CloudWatch** to monitor CPU usage, disk I/O, and memory utilization.

Scale Up or Down:

- Modify instance types (e.g., upgrade from t2.micro to t2.large) in the EC2 dashboard.

Secure Your Server:

- Update your security group to restrict access to known IP addresses.

Real-World Applications

- **E-Commerce**:
  - Hosting scalable platforms for handling high traffic during sales events.
- **Data Processing**:
  - Running batch jobs for analyzing customer data.
- **Development Environments**:

o Hosting virtual servers for collaborative coding and testing.

This chapter introduced the compute services offered by AWS, Azure, and Google Cloud, comparing their features and use cases. Through the real-world example of deploying a virtual server on AWS EC2, you've learned how to create, configure, and manage cloud-based compute resources. These skills are foundational for any cloud-based project, from simple web hosting to complex data processing workflows. In the next chapter, we'll explore serverless computing and how it enables developers to focus solely on code without worrying about infrastructure.

CHAPTER 9: SERVERLESS COMPUTING

Serverless computing is a paradigm shift in cloud computing that allows developers to focus solely on building and running applications without managing infrastructure. It abstracts away server management, enabling applications to scale dynamically based on demand. This chapter explains the fundamentals of serverless architecture, explores offerings from AWS, Azure, and Google Cloud, and walks through a real-world example of building an event-driven notification system.

9.1 Explanation of Serverless Architecture

What Is Serverless Computing?

Serverless computing is a cloud execution model where the cloud provider manages the server infrastructure, dynamically allocates resources, and charges only for the execution time of code.

Key Characteristics

1. **No Server Management**:
   - Developers don't need to provision or maintain servers.
2. **Event-Driven Execution**:
   - Functions are triggered by events, such as HTTP requests, file uploads, or database updates.
3. **Automatic Scaling**:
   - Functions automatically scale based on the number of incoming events.
4. **Pay-as-You-Go**:
   - Billing is based on the number of function executions and the compute time consumed.

Benefits

- **Cost Efficiency**:
  - Pay only for the resources you use, reducing idle costs.
- **Faster Development**:
  - Focus on writing code instead of managing infrastructure.

- **Built-In High Availability**:
  - o Serverless platforms provide redundancy and failover.

Common Use Cases

- Processing file uploads (e.g., image resizing).
- Real-time data streaming and processing.
- Triggering notifications and alerts.
- Running lightweight APIs.

9.2 AWS Lambda, Azure Functions, and Google Cloud Functions

Each major cloud provider offers a robust serverless platform. Let's explore their features and capabilities.

1. AWS Lambda

Overview:

AWS Lambda is a serverless compute service that runs code in response to events. It integrates seamlessly with other AWS services, such as S3, DynamoDB, and API Gateway.

Key Features:

- **Event Sources**:
  - o Triggers include S3 uploads, DynamoDB changes, and API Gateway requests.

- **Runtime Support**:
  - Supports multiple languages, including Python, Node.js, Java, Go, and .NET.
- **Concurrency**:
  - Automatically scales up to handle thousands of requests simultaneously.
- **Timeout**:
  - Maximum execution time of 15 minutes.

Pricing:

- Charges are based on the number of requests and the compute time used.

2. Azure Functions

Overview:

Azure Functions is a serverless compute solution that integrates with the Azure ecosystem, including Event Grid, Cosmos DB, and Logic Apps.

Key Features:

- **Triggers**:
  - Supports HTTP requests, queues, timers, and Azure services like Blob Storage.
- **Durable Functions**:
  - Facilitates orchestration for long-running workflows.

- **Runtime Support**:
    o Languages include C#, Python, JavaScript, Java, and PowerShell.
- **Hybrid Options**:
    o Can run in on-premises environments with Azure Arc.

Pricing:

- Offers a consumption-based plan and premium plans for additional features.

3. Google Cloud Functions

Overview:

Google Cloud Functions is an event-driven, serverless compute platform that integrates well with Google Cloud services like Pub/Sub, Cloud Storage, and Firestore.

Key Features:

- **Event Sources**:
    o Triggers include Cloud Storage events, Pub/Sub messages, and HTTP requests.
- **Runtime Support**:
    o Supports Node.js, Python, Go, Java, and .NET.
- **Global Availability**:

- Functions can run in multiple regions for low latency.
- **Monitoring**:
  - Integrated with Google Cloud Monitoring for tracking function performance.

Pricing:

- Charges are based on invocations, runtime, and outbound data transfer.

9.3 Real-World Example: Building an Event-Driven Notification System

Scenario:

You're tasked with building a notification system for an e-commerce platform. When a user places an order, the system sends an email notification to the user and a text message to the delivery team.

Solution Using Serverless Architecture:

We'll use **AWS Lambda** to build this event-driven system. The workflow involves:

1. An order being placed (event).

2. Lambda functions processing the order and sending notifications.

Steps to Build the Notification System

Step 1: Set Up the Event Source

1. Use **Amazon DynamoDB** as the order database.
2. Create a table named Orders with the following structure:
   - OrderID (Primary Key): Unique identifier for the order.
   - CustomerEmail: Email address of the customer.
   - OrderDetails: JSON object containing order information.

Step 2: Create the Lambda Function

1. Go to the AWS Lambda Console and click **Create Function**.
2. Choose **Author from Scratch** and configure:
   - **Name**: OrderNotificationFunction.
   - **Runtime**: Python 3.x.
3. Write the Lambda code to process the order and send notifications.

Example Code:

```python
import boto3
import json

# Initialize clients for SES (email) and SNS (SMS)
ses = boto3.client('ses')
sns = boto3.client('sns')

def lambda_handler(event, context):
    for record in event['Records']:
        # Extract order details from DynamoDB stream
        order = record['dynamodb']['NewImage']
        email = order['CustomerEmail']['S']
        details = json.loads(order['OrderDetails']['S'])

        # Send email notification
        ses.send_email(
            Source='noreply@myecommerce.com',
            Destination={'ToAddresses': [email]},
            Message={
                'Subject': {'Data': 'Order Confirmation'},
                'Body': {'Text': {'Data': f"Your order {details} has been placed successfully."}}
            }
```

```
)

    # Send SMS notification
    sns.publish(
        PhoneNumber='+1234567890',  # Delivery team number
        Message=f"New order received: {details}"
    )
    return {'statusCode': 200, 'body': 'Notifications sent
successfully'}
```

Step 3: Configure the Trigger

1. Enable DynamoDB Streams for the Orders table.
2. Set the Lambda function as the event source for the stream:
   - Choose **Trigger** → **DynamoDB** → Select Orders → Enable **New and Old Image**.

Step 4: Test the System

1. Insert a new order into the Orders table using the AWS Console or CLI.

bash

```
aws dynamodb put-item --table-name Orders \
```

--item '{"OrderID": {"S": "12345"}, "CustomerEmail": {"S": "customer@example.com"}, "OrderDetails": {"S": "{\"item\": \"Laptop\", \"price\": 1200}"}}'

2. Confirm that:

   o The customer receives an order confirmation email.

   o The delivery team receives an SMS with order details.

Outcome

Using AWS Lambda, SES, and SNS, the event-driven notification system is:

- **Scalable**: Handles increasing order volumes without additional configuration.
- **Cost-Efficient**: Charges only for the resources used during function execution.
- **Easy to Manage**: No server maintenance or scaling required.

Serverless computing empowers developers to build scalable, event-driven applications without the burden of managing infrastructure. In this chapter, we explored the fundamentals of serverless architecture, the serverless offerings from AWS, Azure, and Google Cloud, and implemented a real-world example of a notification system. These concepts pave the way for leveraging serverless solutions in complex applications, enabling faster development and cost efficiency. In the next chapter, we'll explore networking in the cloud, focusing on how to securely and efficiently connect resources.

CHAPTER 10: CLOUD NETWORKING

Networking is the backbone of cloud infrastructure, enabling resources to communicate securely and efficiently. Cloud providers offer powerful networking tools that give you control over IP addresses, subnets, firewalls, and traffic routing. This chapter introduces the basics of cloud networking with a focus on VPCs (Virtual Private Clouds) in AWS, Azure, and Google Cloud, and explores managing IPs, subnets, and load balancers. It concludes with a real-world example of setting up a secure, multi-region application.

10.1 Basics of Cloud Networking

1. Virtual Private Cloud (AWS)
Overview:

Amazon VPC (Virtual Private Cloud) allows you to define a logically isolated network within AWS. It gives you full control over your networking environment, including IP address ranges, subnets, and routing.

Key Features:

- **Subnets**: Divide your VPC into public and private subnets.
- **Security**: Configure security groups and network access control lists (ACLs).
- **Internet Gateway (IGW)**: Connects your VPC to the internet.
- **NAT Gateway**: Allows private instances to access the internet without being directly exposed.

Use Cases:

- Hosting multi-tier web applications.
- Building secure environments for data processing.

2. Virtual Network (Azure)

Overview:

Azure Virtual Network (VNet) is the equivalent of AWS VPC, providing isolated networking environments for Azure resources. VNets can be connected to on-premises data centers using VPN gateways or ExpressRoute.

Key Features:

- **Subnets**: Organize resources into public or private subnets.
- **Peering**: Connect VNets across different regions or subscriptions.
- **Network Security Groups (NSGs)**: Control traffic to resources within the VNet.
- **Integration**: Seamlessly integrates with Azure services like App Service and Azure Kubernetes Service (AKS).

Use Cases:

- Extending on-premises networks to the cloud.
- Creating hybrid or multi-cloud environments.

3. Virtual Private Cloud (Google Cloud)

Overview:

Google Cloud VPC provides a scalable and global networking solution, allowing resources to communicate securely across regions and zones.

Key Features:

- **Global Networking**: A single VPC spans multiple regions, reducing complexity.
- **Subnets**: Automatically created when resources are provisioned in a region.
- **Firewall Rules**: Control inbound and outbound traffic.
- **Cloud Interconnect**: Connects your VPC to on-premises networks with high bandwidth.

Use Cases:

- Deploying global applications with low latency.
- Building secure, multi-region architectures.

10.2 Managing IPs, Subnets, and Load Balancers

1. IP Address Management
Private IPs:

- Used within a VPC or VNet for internal communication.
- Not accessible from the internet.

Public IPs:

- Assigned to resources like virtual machines or load balancers for external access.

Elastic IPs (AWS):

- Static public IPs that can be reassigned between instances.

Reserved IPs (Azure & Google Cloud):

- Assign static IPs for predictable addressing.

2. Subnets
Public Subnets:

- Resources in these subnets can communicate with the internet (e.g., web servers).

Private Subnets:

- Resources in these subnets are isolated from the internet and used for backend systems like databases.

Subnet Best Practices:

1. Assign separate subnets for different application tiers (web, app, database).
2. Use smaller CIDR blocks to conserve IP addresses.

3. Load Balancers

Load balancers distribute incoming traffic across multiple resources to ensure high availability and fault tolerance.

AWS Elastic Load Balancer (ELB):

- **Types**: Application Load Balancer (HTTP/HTTPS), Network Load Balancer (TCP/UDP), and Gateway Load Balancer.

Azure Load Balancer:

- Supports internal and public load balancing with health probes.

Google Cloud Load Balancer:

- Provides global and regional load balancing for HTTP(S), TCP, and SSL traffic.

10.3 Real-World Example: Setting Up a Secure, Multi-Region Application

Scenario:

You need to deploy a global e-commerce application with the following requirements:

1. **Multi-Region Availability**: Application must serve users from different geographic locations.

2. **Secure Communication**: Resources should be protected from unauthorized access.

3. **Scalable Backend**: Automatically scale resources based on demand.

Solution Using AWS VPC

Step 1: Create a Multi-Region VPC

1. **Region Selection**:
   o Create a VPC in two AWS regions (e.g., us-east-1 and eu-west-1).
2. **CIDR Block Assignment**:
   o Assign 10.0.0.0/16 for the VPC in us-east-1.
   o Assign 10.1.0.0/16 for the VPC in eu-west-1.

Step 2: Create Subnets

1. In each region, create:
   o **Public Subnet** for web servers (e.g., 10.0.1.0/24 in us-east-1).
   o **Private Subnet** for databases (e.g., 10.0.2.0/24 in us-east-1).
2. Enable auto-assign public IPs for instances in public subnets.

Step 3: Configure Security

1. **Security Groups**:
   - Allow HTTP (port 80) and HTTPS (port 443) traffic for web servers.
   - Restrict database access to the private subnet only.
2. **NACLs**:
   - Define rules to block unauthorized IP ranges.

Step 4: Deploy Load Balancers

1. Create an **Application Load Balancer** in each region:
   - Target group: Auto Scaling group for web servers.
   - Enable health checks for instance monitoring.
2. Use **Route 53** for DNS:
   - Configure geolocation routing to direct users to the nearest region.

Step 5: Set Up Database Replication

1. Deploy an **RDS instance** in each region.
2. Enable **Cross-Region Replication** to synchronize data between regions.

Step 6: Test and Monitor

1. Use **AWS CloudWatch** to monitor network traffic and instance health.
2. Simulate regional failures to ensure automatic failover.

Outcome

The multi-region e-commerce application provides:

- **High Availability**: Traffic is routed to the nearest healthy region.
- **Scalability**: Resources automatically scale to handle peak traffic.
- **Security**: Public-facing resources are isolated from private systems.

In this chapter, we explored the fundamentals of cloud networking, focusing on VPCs and networking services across AWS, Azure, and Google Cloud. We covered how to manage IPs, subnets, and load balancers, and demonstrated a real-world example of deploying a secure, multi-region application. Networking is a critical component of cloud architecture, enabling secure and efficient communication across resources. In the next chapter, we'll dive into cloud databases, exploring relational and NoSQL offerings.

CHAPTER 11: CLOUD DATABASES

Databases are the cornerstone of virtually every application, from e-commerce platforms to analytics dashboards. Cloud providers offer powerful database solutions that combine scalability, high availability, and integrated tools for seamless management. This chapter introduces relational and NoSQL databases in the cloud, explores key offerings like AWS RDS, Azure SQL Database, and Google Cloud SQL, and walks through a real-world example of migrating a database to the cloud.

11.1 Introduction to Relational and NoSQL Databases in the Cloud

1. Relational Databases

Overview:

Relational databases organize data into tables with predefined schemas. They use SQL (Structured Query Language) to manage and query data.

Key Characteristics:

- **Structured Schema**: Data must conform to a defined schema.
- **ACID Compliance**: Ensures data consistency through atomicity, consistency, isolation, and durability.
- **Use Cases**:
  - o Financial systems.
  - o Inventory management.
  - o Applications requiring complex queries and transactions.

Examples:

- MySQL, PostgreSQL, SQL Server, Oracle.

2. NoSQL Databases

Overview:

NoSQL databases are designed for unstructured or semi-structured data. They offer flexibility and scalability, making them ideal for modern applications with dynamic requirements.

Key Characteristics:

- **Schema-Less**: Data can be stored without a fixed schema.
- **Horizontal Scalability**: Designed to scale across multiple servers.
- **Types**:
  - **Document Stores**: MongoDB, CouchDB.
  - **Key-Value Stores**: DynamoDB, Redis.
  - **Column Stores**: Cassandra, HBase.
  - **Graph Databases**: Neo4j, Amazon Neptune.
- **Use Cases**:
  - Real-time analytics.
  - IoT applications.
  - Social media platforms.

Why Use Cloud Databases?

- **Managed Services**: Providers handle backups, updates, and scaling.
- **Global Accessibility**: Deploy databases close to your users for low-latency access.
- **Cost Efficiency**: Pay only for the resources you use, with no need to manage hardware.

11.2 AWS RDS, Azure SQL Database, and Google Cloud SQL

1. AWS RDS (Relational Database Service)

Overview:

AWS RDS is a fully managed service for relational databases, supporting engines like MySQL, PostgreSQL, MariaDB, Oracle, and SQL Server.

Key Features:

- **Automated Backups**: Daily backups with point-in-time recovery.
- **Multi-AZ Deployments**: Ensures high availability by replicating data across availability zones.
- **Read Replicas**: Scale read operations by creating read-only replicas.
- **Integration**: Seamlessly integrates with AWS services like Lambda and CloudWatch.

Use Cases:

- E-commerce platforms requiring high availability.
- ERP systems needing complex transactions.

2. Azure SQL Database

Overview:

Azure SQL Database is a fully managed relational database as a service (DBaaS) based on Microsoft SQL Server.

Key Features:

- **Built-In AI**: Automatically optimizes performance using AI.
- **Elastic Pools**: Share resources across multiple databases for cost savings.
- **Global Scalability**: Supports geo-replication to distribute data worldwide.
- **Advanced Security**: Offers encryption, auditing, and compliance with standards like GDPR.

Use Cases:

- Applications already integrated with Microsoft services.
- SaaS applications requiring elastic scalability.

3. Google Cloud SQL

Overview:

Google Cloud SQL is a managed service for relational databases like MySQL, PostgreSQL, and SQL Server.

Key Features:

- **High Availability**: Automatic failover and data replication.
- **Sustained-Use Discounts**: Cost savings for long-running workloads.
- **Integration with BigQuery**: Enables seamless analytics on relational data.
- **Scalability**: Vertical and horizontal scaling with minimal downtime.

Use Cases:

- Real-time analytics combined with BigQuery.
- Web applications with frequent user queries.

Comparison of Key Features

Feature	AWS RDS	Azure SQL Database	Google Cloud SQL
Supported Engines	MySQL, PostgreSQL,	SQL Server	MySQL, PostgreSQL, SQL

Feature	AWS RDS	Azure SQL Database	Google Cloud SQL
		etc.	
High Availability	Multi-AZ	Geo-Replication	Automatic Failover
Scaling	Read Replicas	Elastic Pools	Vertical/Horizontal
Integration	AWS Ecosystem	Microsoft Ecosystem	Google Ecosystem
Security	IAM, Encryption	Advanced Security Features	Data Encryption

11.3 Real-World Example: Migrating a Database to the Cloud

Scenario:

A retail company wants to migrate its on-premises MySQL database to AWS RDS. The goals are:

- High availability and automatic backups.
- Scalability to handle seasonal spikes in traffic.
- Minimal downtime during the migration.

Steps to Migrate the Database

Step 1: Prepare the On-Premises Database

1. **Backup Data**:
   - Export the database using mysqldump:

   bash

   mysqldump -u root -p my_database > backup.sql

2. **Assess Compatibility**:
   - Use the AWS Schema Conversion Tool (SCT) to ensure compatibility between the on-premises schema and RDS.

Step 2: Create an RDS Instance

1. Log in to the AWS Management Console.
2. Navigate to **RDS** and click **Create Database**.
3. Choose **Standard Create** and configure:
   - **Engine**: MySQL.
   - **Instance Class**: db.t3.micro (Free Tier eligible).
   - **Multi-AZ Deployment**: Enabled.
   - **Storage**: 20 GB General Purpose SSD.
4. Configure credentials (e.g., master username and password).
5. Launch the RDS instance.

Step 3: Import Data into RDS

1. Connect to the RDS instance:

bash

```
mysql -h <rds-endpoint> -u admin -p
```

2. Import the backup:

bash

```
mysql -h <rds-endpoint> -u admin -p my_database < backup.sql
```

Step 4: Update the Application

1. Update the application's database connection string to point to the RDS endpoint:

python

```
DATABASE_HOST = '<rds-endpoint>'
DATABASE_USER = 'admin'
DATABASE_PASSWORD = 'password'
DATABASE_NAME = 'my_database'
```

Step 5: Test and Optimize

1. Test the application to ensure proper functionality.

2. Monitor the database using **CloudWatch** to track performance metrics like CPU usage and query times.

Step 6: Enable Backups and Monitoring

1. Configure automated backups in the RDS console.
2. Set up alarms for high CPU usage or storage thresholds.

Outcome:

The retail company successfully migrates its database to AWS RDS, achieving:

- **High Availability**: Multi-AZ deployment ensures minimal downtime.
- **Scalability**: Read replicas handle increased traffic during seasonal sales.
- **Operational Efficiency**: Automated backups and monitoring reduce maintenance overhead.

Cloud databases offer powerful, managed solutions for storing and processing data, catering to both relational and NoSQL needs. In this chapter, we explored relational and NoSQL databases, focusing on AWS RDS, Azure SQL Database, and Google Cloud SQL. Through the example of migrating a database to AWS RDS, you've seen how cloud databases simplify operations, improve availability, and scale dynamically. In the next chapter, we'll delve into monitoring and logging tools, ensuring you can track and optimize cloud resources effectively.

CHAPTER 12: MONITORING AND LOGGING

Monitoring and logging are critical for maintaining the health, performance, and security of cloud-based applications. They enable organizations to identify potential issues, optimize resource utilization, and ensure system reliability. This chapter explores the importance of monitoring and logging in the cloud, examines tools like AWS CloudWatch, Azure Monitor, and Google Cloud Operations Suite, and walks through a real-world example of troubleshooting performance issues using logs.

12.1 Importance of Monitoring and Logging in the Cloud

Why Monitoring and Logging Are Essential

1. **Visibility**:
    o   Provides real-time insights into the performance and status of cloud resources.
    o   Detects unusual behavior or performance degradation.

2. **Proactive Issue Resolution**:
    o   Alerts and notifications help resolve problems before they impact users.
    o   Logs enable root-cause analysis after incidents occur.

3. **Optimization**:
   - Helps optimize resource usage by identifying underutilized or overburdened services.
   - Tracks cost implications and supports budgeting efforts.

4. **Compliance and Security**:
   - Logs provide an audit trail for compliance with regulations like GDPR or HIPAA.
   - Helps identify potential security threats or unauthorized access.

5. **Scalability and Reliability**:
   - Monitoring ensures systems scale effectively under increased workloads.
   - Identifies and addresses reliability issues to maintain uptime.

Key Components of Monitoring and Logging

1. **Metrics**:
   - Quantitative measurements (e.g., CPU usage, memory utilization, network latency).

2. **Logs**:
   - Detailed records of events, errors, and transactions within systems.

3. **Alerts**:

o Notifications triggered when metrics or logs exceed predefined thresholds.

4. **Dashboards**:

   o Visual interfaces summarizing metrics and log data for easy analysis.

12.2 AWS CloudWatch, Azure Monitor, and Google Cloud Operations Suite

1. AWS CloudWatch

Overview:

AWS CloudWatch is a monitoring and observability service that collects and analyzes metrics, logs, and events from AWS resources and applications.

Key Features:

- **Metrics**:
    o Monitors CPU usage, disk I/O, and network activity for EC2 instances.
- **Logs**:
    o Collects logs from AWS services like Lambda, RDS, and ECS.
- **Alarms**:
    o Sends alerts when metrics exceed thresholds (e.g., high memory usage).
- **Custom Dashboards**:

- o Create dashboards to visualize real-time data.
- **Integration**:
  - o Works seamlessly with AWS Lambda, SNS, and other AWS tools.

Example Use Case:

- Monitor the performance of a web application running on EC2 and trigger alerts when latency exceeds 500 ms.

2. Azure Monitor

Overview:

Azure Monitor provides end-to-end monitoring for Azure resources, applications, and networks.

Key Features:

- **Metrics and Logs**:
  - o Tracks performance and diagnostic data for VMs, databases, and other resources.
- **Application Insights**:
  - o Offers deep insights into application performance and user behavior.
- **Alerts**:
  - o Provides actionable alerts based on custom conditions.
- **Log Analytics**:

o   Allows querying logs using KQL (Kusto Query Language).

- **Integration**:
  o   Connects with Power BI for advanced visualization.

Example Use Case:

- Use Application Insights to monitor an Azure-hosted API for response times and failure rates.

3. Google Cloud Operations Suite

Overview:

Formerly known as Stackdriver, Google Cloud Operations Suite provides monitoring, logging, and tracing capabilities for Google Cloud resources and hybrid environments.

Key Features:

- **Monitoring**:
  o   Collects metrics from Compute Engine, Kubernetes Engine, and Cloud Functions.
- **Logging**:
  o   Centralized log collection for analyzing system and application logs.
- **Tracing**:
  o   Provides detailed latency breakdowns for distributed applications.

- **Dashboards**:
  - Customizable dashboards for visualizing performance metrics.
- **Integration**:
  - Works with third-party tools like PagerDuty and Slack for notifications.

Example Use Case:

- Monitor a Kubernetes cluster for resource usage and application performance, with detailed tracing for slow API endpoints.

Comparison of Tools

Feature	AWS CloudWatch	Azure Monitor	Google Cloud Operations Suite
Metrics and Logs	Comprehensive AWS focus	Strong integration with Azure	Cross-platform (hybrid support)
Custom Dashboards	Yes	Yes	Yes
Alerting	Threshold-based	Threshold-	Threshold-based

Feature	AWS CloudWatch	Azure Monitor	Google Cloud Operations Suite
		based	
Integration	AWS services	Microsoft ecosystem	Google Cloud services
Unique Strength	Detailed alarms	Application Insights	Tracing and latency analysis

12.3 Real-World Example: Troubleshooting Performance Issues Using Logs

Scenario:

A video streaming service experiences intermittent buffering issues for users. The system includes:

- **Frontend**: Web application hosted on Google Cloud.
- **Backend**: API running on Compute Engine instances.
- **Database**: Cloud SQL.

The objective is to identify and resolve the root cause of performance degradation.

Steps to Troubleshoot Using Google Cloud Operations Suite

Step 1: Collect Metrics and Logs

1. Enable **Cloud Monitoring**:
   - Set up metrics collection for Compute Engine instances (CPU, memory, network usage).
2. Enable **Cloud Logging**:
   - Collect logs from the API service for incoming requests and errors.

Step 2: Analyze Metrics

1. Open the **Cloud Monitoring Dashboard**:
   - View CPU and memory usage for Compute Engine instances.
   - Identify spikes in resource utilization during buffering incidents.
2. Network Metrics:
   - Analyze incoming and outgoing traffic to detect bottlenecks.

Observation:

- High CPU utilization during peak traffic suggests the backend is overloaded.

Step 3: Query Logs

1. Use **Log Explorer**:
   o Search for errors in the API logs using filters:

   text

   resource.type="gce_instance"
   severity="ERROR"

2. Analyze patterns:
   o Identify errors related to slow database queries or timeouts.

Observation:

- Logs show repeated database query timeouts, pointing to a potential issue with the Cloud SQL instance.

Step 4: Resolve the Issue

1. **Database Optimization**:
   o Index frequently queried columns in the database to improve performance.
2. **Scale Backend Instances**:

o Use Compute Engine autoscaling to handle increased traffic.

Step 5: Monitor the Solution

1. Set up Alerts:
   o Configure alerts for high CPU usage or database query latencies exceeding 100 ms.
2. Test Performance:
   o Simulate high traffic to ensure the system handles load effectively.

Outcome:

- Buffering issues are resolved by optimizing the database and scaling the backend.
- Ongoing monitoring ensures quick detection of future performance problems.

Monitoring and logging are indispensable for managing cloud-based systems effectively. Tools like AWS CloudWatch, Azure Monitor, and Google Cloud Operations Suite provide comprehensive capabilities to track metrics, collect logs, and set up alerts. Through the real-world example of troubleshooting a video streaming service, you've seen how these tools can identify and resolve performance issues. In the next chapter, we'll explore the importance of cloud security and how to secure your applications and data.

CHAPTER 13: CLOUD SECURITY BASICS

Security is a fundamental aspect of cloud computing, safeguarding data, applications, and infrastructure from unauthorized access and cyber threats. Cloud providers emphasize a **shared responsibility model** to clarify the division of security tasks between the provider and the customer. This chapter explores cloud security fundamentals, introduces tools like AWS IAM, Azure Active Directory, and Google Cloud IAM, and walks through a real-world example of configuring user roles and permissions.

13.1 Shared Responsibility Model in Cloud Security

What Is the Shared Responsibility Model?

Cloud security operates under a shared responsibility model, where:

- **The Cloud Provider**: Secures the infrastructure, including hardware, software, networking, and physical data centers.
- **The Customer**: Secures their data, applications, and access configurations within the cloud environment.

Responsibility Breakdown by Service Model

1. **Infrastructure as a Service (IaaS)**:
   - Provider: Manages physical security, networking, and virtualization layers.
   - Customer: Manages operating systems, applications, and access controls.

2. **Platform as a Service (PaaS)**:
   - Provider: Secures the platform, including runtime and middleware.
   - Customer: Secures application code, data, and user permissions.

3. **Software as a Service (SaaS)**:
   - Provider: Manages everything, including applications.
   - Customer: Ensures proper access controls and data integrity.

Benefits of the Shared Responsibility Model

- **Clarity**: Clearly defines security roles for providers and customers.
- **Collaboration**: Encourages customers and providers to work together to secure systems.
- **Scalability**: Allows customers to focus on securing their workloads without managing infrastructure.

13.2 Security Tools in Cloud Platforms

1. AWS Identity and Access Management (IAM)

Overview:

AWS IAM is a tool for managing access to AWS resources. It enables customers to control who can perform specific actions on which resources.

Key Features:

- **Users and Groups**: Create individual users and group them to apply permissions collectively.
- **Roles**: Assign temporary access permissions for resources.
- **Policies**: JSON-based documents defining permissions (e.g., read-only access to S3).
- **MFA (Multi-Factor Authentication)**: Adds an extra layer of security.

Example Use Case:

- Restrict access to an S3 bucket to specific users while enabling read-only public access for certain objects.

2. Azure Active Directory (Azure AD)

Overview:

Azure AD is a cloud-based identity and access management solution integrated with Microsoft Azure and Office 365.

Key Features:

- **Single Sign-On (SSO)**: Allows users to log in once and access multiple applications.
- **Conditional Access**: Enforces policies based on user roles, locations, or devices.
- **Role-Based Access Control (RBAC)**: Assigns permissions based on predefined roles.
- **Integration**: Works seamlessly with on-premises Active Directory.

Example Use Case:

- Configure conditional access to block sign-ins from non-corporate devices while allowing secure access for remote workers.

3. Google Cloud Identity and Access Management (IAM)

Overview:

Google Cloud IAM provides fine-grained access control for GCP resources, allowing customers to enforce the principle of least privilege.

Key Features:

- **Resource Hierarchy**: Organizes resources into projects, folders, and organizations for structured access control.
- **Predefined Roles**: Built-in roles for common tasks (e.g., Compute Engine Admin).
- **Custom Roles**: Create roles with specific permissions tailored to organizational needs.
- **Audit Logs**: Tracks access and changes for compliance.

Example Use Case:

- Grant a developer access to deploy applications on Compute Engine without allowing them to delete resources.

13.3 Real-World Example: Configuring User Roles and Permissions

Scenario:

A company wants to configure secure access to its cloud resources for a team of developers, ensuring:

1. Developers can manage and deploy resources in a development environment.
2. Developers have read-only access to the production environment.
3. Admins have full access to all environments.

Solution Using AWS IAM

Step 1: Define Requirements

1. **Development Environment**:
   o Allow full access to developers for creating and managing resources.
2. **Production Environment**:
   o Grant read-only access to developers.
   o Grant full access to admins.

Step 2: Create IAM Groups

1. **Developer Group**:
   o Assign permissions to manage resources in the development environment.
2. **Admin Group**:
   o Assign permissions to manage all resources across environments.

Step 3: Define IAM Policies Create two custom policies using JSON:

1. **Developer Policy (Development Access)**:

   json

```
{
    "Version": "2012-10-17",
```

```json
    "Statement": [
      {
        "Effect": "Allow",
        "Action": "ec2:*",
        "Resource":              "arn:aws:ec2:region:account-
id:instance/*"
      }
    ]
}
```

2. **Read-Only Policy (Production Access)**:

json

```json
{
  "Version": "2012-10-17",
  "Statement": [
    {
      "Effect": "Allow",
      "Action": [
        "ec2:Describe*",
        "s3:Get*"
      ],
      "Resource": "*"
    }
  ]
```

}

Step 4: Assign Policies to Groups

1. Attach the **Developer Policy** to the **Developer Group**.
2. Attach the **Read-Only Policy** to the **Developer Group** for production access.
3. Attach full-access policies (e.g., AdministratorAccess) to the **Admin Group**.

Step 5: Create Users and Assign Groups

1. Add individual team members as IAM users.
2. Assign users to the appropriate groups:
    - Developers → Developer Group.
    - Admins → Admin Group.

Step 6: Enable Multi-Factor Authentication

1. Require MFA for all users.
2. Configure MFA in the IAM Console and guide users through setup.

Step 7: Test and Verify

1. Log in as a developer:
    - Verify full access to the development environment.

      o   Ensure only read-only access to the production environment.

2. Log in as an admin:
   - Verify unrestricted access across all resources.

Outcome

- Developers can securely manage the development environment while maintaining limited access to production.
- Admins have complete control over resources.
- MFA ensures secure authentication, reducing the risk of unauthorized access.

Cloud security is a collaborative effort between providers and customers under the shared responsibility model. Tools like AWS IAM, Azure Active Directory, and Google Cloud IAM empower organizations to enforce granular access control and secure their cloud environments. Through the example of configuring user roles and permissions, this chapter demonstrated practical steps for implementing secure access policies. In the next chapter, we'll delve into backup and disaster recovery strategies, ensuring data resilience in the cloud.

CHAPTER 14: BACKUP AND DISASTER RECOVERY

Backup and disaster recovery (DR) are critical components of any cloud strategy, ensuring data availability and operational continuity in the face of unforeseen failures, cyberattacks, or natural disasters. Cloud platforms offer robust tools to simplify backups and recovery processes, enabling businesses to safeguard their assets and recover quickly. This chapter explores the fundamentals of cloud backups and disaster recovery, examines tools like AWS Backup, Azure Site Recovery, and Google Cloud Backup, and walks through a real-world example of designing a backup plan for a small business.

14.1 Implementing Cloud Backups and Disaster Recovery Strategies

1. Importance of Backups and Disaster Recovery

- **Data Protection**:

o Ensures critical data is securely stored and recoverable after accidental deletion, corruption, or cyberattacks.

- **Business Continuity**:
  o Minimizes downtime by enabling rapid recovery of systems.
- **Compliance**:
  o Meets regulatory requirements for data retention and recovery (e.g., GDPR, HIPAA).
- **Cost Efficiency**:
  o Cloud solutions eliminate the need for physical storage, reducing costs and improving scalability.

2. Backup Strategies

1. **Full Backup**:
   o Captures the entire dataset in each backup cycle.
   o Pros: Comprehensive and simple recovery process.
   o Cons: Time-consuming and storage-intensive.
2. **Incremental Backup**:
   o Backs up only the data that has changed since the last backup.
   o Pros: Efficient in storage and time.
   o Cons: Recovery involves restoring from multiple backup points.
3. **Differential Backup**:

- o Backs up data changed since the last full backup.
- o Pros: Faster recovery than incremental backups.
- o Cons: Requires more storage than incremental backups.

4. **Snapshot-Based Backup**:
   - o Captures the state of a system or database at a specific moment.
   - o Pros: Fast and ideal for virtualized environments.
   - o Cons: May require integration with other tools for long-term retention.

3. Disaster Recovery Strategies

1. **Cold Site**:
   - o Minimal infrastructure available for recovery; systems need to be rebuilt.
   - o Pros: Cost-effective.
   - o Cons: High downtime during recovery.

2. **Warm Site**:
   - o Partially configured infrastructure with some services running.
   - o Pros: Faster recovery than a cold site.
   - o Cons: More expensive than a cold site.

3. **Hot Site**:
   - o Fully configured and running infrastructure, mirroring the primary environment.

- o   Pros: Minimal downtime.
- o   Cons: High cost.

4. **Pilot Light**:

- o   A small subset of critical services running in the backup environment.
- o   Pros: Balances cost and recovery time.

5. **Active-Active**:

- o   Fully redundant systems in multiple locations that run simultaneously.
- o   Pros: Near-zero downtime.
- o   Cons: Expensive and complex to manage.

14.2 AWS Backup, Azure Site Recovery, and Google Cloud Backup

1. AWS Backup

Overview:

AWS Backup centralizes and automates backup management for AWS services like EC2, RDS, DynamoDB, and S3.

Key Features:

- **Backup Policies**: Define schedules, retention periods, and lifecycle rules.
- **Cross-Region Backup**: Automatically replicate backups to different regions for disaster recovery.

- **Integration**: Works seamlessly with AWS services and on-premises workloads.

Use Cases:

- Regular backups of databases and file systems.
- Cross-region disaster recovery for critical applications.

2. Azure Site Recovery

Overview:

Azure Site Recovery (ASR) replicates workloads running on virtual or physical machines to Azure, enabling seamless disaster recovery.

Key Features:

- **Replication**: Supports replication of VMs, on-premises servers, and cloud workloads.
- **Failover and Failback**: Automates failover to Azure and failback to the primary environment.
- **Compliance**: Meets RPO (Recovery Point Objective) and RTO (Recovery Time Objective) targets.

Use Cases:

- Disaster recovery for hybrid environments.
- Migration of on-premises systems to Azure.

3. Google Cloud Backup

Overview:

Google Cloud Backup and DR provides policy-based management for backups of databases, VMs, and applications.

Key Features:

- **Unified Console**: Manage backups across multiple Google Cloud services.
- **Snapshots**: Create point-in-time snapshots of Compute Engine and persistent disks.
- **Regional and Multi-Regional**: Store backups in geographically distributed locations.

Use Cases:

- Backup and restore GCP VMs and applications.
- Disaster recovery for Kubernetes clusters.

Comparison of Tools

Feature	AWS Backup	Azure Site Recovery	Google Cloud Backup
Backup Scope	AWS services, on-prem	VMs, servers, cloud workloads	Databases, VMs, Kubernetes apps

Feature	AWS Backup	Azure Site Recovery	Google Cloud Backup
Disaster Recovery	Cross-region replication	Automated failover/failback	Regional and multi-regional DR
Automation	Policy-based	Policy-based	Policy-based
Integration	AWS ecosystem	Microsoft ecosystem	Google Cloud ecosystem

14.3 Real-World Example: Designing a Backup Plan for a Small Business

Scenario:

A small business runs a web application hosted on an AWS EC2 instance with an RDS database. The business wants to:

1. Protect its data from accidental loss or ransomware attacks.
2. Ensure application availability in case of hardware or regional failure.

Solution Using AWS Backup

Step 1: Define Requirements

1. **Backup Scope**:
   - o EC2 instance (web application server).
   - o RDS database (application data).
2. **Retention Policy**:
   - o Retain daily backups for 30 days.
3. **Disaster Recovery**:
   - o Store backups in a secondary AWS region for redundancy.

Step 2: Set Up AWS Backup

1. **Create a Backup Plan**:
   - o Go to the AWS Backup Console.
   - o Click **Create Backup Plan**.
   - o Configure:
     - **Backup Frequency**: Daily.
     - **Retention Period**: 30 days.
     - **Lifecycle Rules**: Transition to cold storage after 15 days.
2. **Assign Resources**:
   - o Add the EC2 instance and RDS database to the backup plan.

Step 3: Enable Cross-Region Backup

1. Configure backup policies to replicate backups to a secondary region (e.g., us-west-2).

2. Test replication to ensure backups are available in both regions.

Step 4: Test Disaster Recovery

1. **Simulate Failover**:
   - Launch a new EC2 instance using a backup AMI.
   - Restore the RDS database from the latest snapshot.
2. Verify that the application works as expected.

Step 5: Monitor and Optimize

1. Use AWS Backup reports to track backup status and storage costs.
2. Set up CloudWatch alarms for failed backups or high storage usage.

Outcome

- The small business achieves a robust backup strategy with automated daily backups and cross-region disaster recovery.
- The solution ensures data availability, meets compliance requirements, and minimizes downtime in case of failure.

Backup and disaster recovery strategies are essential for ensuring data protection and business continuity. Cloud providers like AWS, Azure, and Google Cloud offer comprehensive tools to automate and simplify these processes. Through the real-world example of designing a backup plan for a small business, this chapter demonstrated practical steps to implement reliable and cost-effective cloud backups and disaster recovery solutions. In the next chapter, we'll explore the use of cloud databases and their role in managing semi-structured and unstructured data.

CHAPTER 15: COST MANAGEMENT IN THE CLOUD

Cost management is a critical aspect of cloud computing. While cloud platforms offer scalability and flexibility, without proper oversight, expenses can escalate quickly. This chapter delves into cost optimization techniques, highlights tools like AWS Cost Explorer, Azure Cost Management, and Google Cloud Billing, and walks through a real-world example of reducing costs for a test environment.

15.1 Cost Optimization Techniques

Effective cost management requires understanding cloud expenses and implementing strategies to minimize unnecessary costs. Below are key techniques:

1. Monitor and Analyze Usage

- Regularly review resource utilization to identify underutilized or idle resources.
- Use billing reports to understand spending trends.

2. Right-Sizing Resources

- Choose the optimal instance size or service configuration for your workload.
  - Example: Downgrade an EC2 instance from m5.large to t3.micro if it consistently operates below capacity.

3. Leverage Reserved Instances and Savings Plans

- Purchase Reserved Instances (RIs) for predictable workloads to save up to 75%.
- Use Savings Plans for flexibility across instance families and regions.

4. Enable Auto-Scaling

- Configure auto-scaling to dynamically adjust resources based on demand.
  - o Example: Scale down during off-peak hours to reduce costs.

5. Use Spot or Preemptible Instances

- For non-critical workloads, leverage discounted Spot Instances (AWS) or Preemptible VMs (Google Cloud).
  - o Example: Run batch processing jobs with Spot Instances to save up to 90%.

6. Optimize Storage

- Transition infrequently accessed data to lower-cost storage tiers:
  - o AWS S3 Glacier, Azure Cool Storage, or Google Coldline Storage.
- Enable data lifecycle policies to automate transitions.

7. Implement Governance and Alerts

- Set budgets and configure alerts for exceeding thresholds.
- Use tagging policies to track expenses by project or team.

8. Use Serverless Architectures

- Serverless solutions like AWS Lambda or Google Cloud Functions eliminate idle costs by billing only for execution time.

15.2 Tools for Cloud Cost Management

1. AWS Cost Explorer

Overview:

AWS Cost Explorer provides detailed insights into AWS spending patterns and resource utilization.

Key Features:

- **Spend Analysis**:
  - View historical data and identify cost drivers.
- **Forecasting**:
  - Predict future expenses based on usage trends.
- **Savings Plans**:
  - Analyze savings opportunities for Reserved Instances and Savings Plans.
- **Resource Grouping**:
  - Break down costs by project, service, or tags.

Use Case:

- A startup monitors its EC2 costs and identifies savings by migrating non-critical workloads to Spot Instances.

2. Azure Cost Management

Overview:

Azure Cost Management offers tools to monitor, allocate, and optimize Azure spending.

Key Features:

- **Budgeting and Alerts**:
  - o Set budgets and receive alerts when costs approach limits.
- **Cost Allocation**:
  - o Use tags to allocate costs to teams or departments.
- **Recommendations**:
  - o Suggests optimizations like resizing VMs or leveraging Reserved Instances.
- **Multi-Cloud Support**:
  - o Monitor costs across Azure and AWS.

Use Case:

- An enterprise uses tagging to track expenses by department and implements recommendations to optimize VM usage.

3. Google Cloud Billing

Overview:

Google Cloud Billing provides visibility and control over GCP costs with real-time insights.

Key Features:

- **Budgets and Notifications**:
  - Set up budgets with automated notifications for threshold breaches.
- **Detailed Reports**:
  - Break down costs by service, region, or project.
- **Committed Use Discounts**:
  - Save costs on predictable workloads with committed use contracts.
- **Billing Export**:
  - Export billing data to BigQuery for advanced analysis.

Use Case:

- A data analytics company uses billing exports and BigQuery to analyze usage trends and reduce costs on idle VMs.

Comparison of Tools

Feature	AWS Cost Explorer	Azure Cost Management	Google Cloud Billing
Spend	Detailed usage	Service	and Service,

Feature	AWS Cost Explorer	Azure Cost Management	Google Cloud Billing
Analysis	insights	department views	region, and project views
Budgeting	Alerts and recommendations	Budgets with alerts	Budgets with notifications
Optimization Guidance	Savings Plans and RIs	VM and service recommendations	Committed use discounts
Multi-Cloud Support	AWS-specific	Supports Azure and AWS	Google Cloud-specific

15.3 Real-World Example: Reducing Costs for a Test Environment

Scenario:

A software development team runs a test environment in AWS, including:

- Three m5.large EC2 instances for application testing.

- 500 GB of Amazon S3 Standard storage for logs and backups.
- An RDS instance for the test database.

The team wants to reduce costs without affecting performance.

Solution Using AWS Cost Management

Step 1: Monitor Usage

1. Use **AWS Cost Explorer** to analyze resource utilization:
   - Identify underutilized EC2 instances with low CPU and memory usage.
   - Check S3 storage trends and identify rarely accessed files.

Step 2: Right-Size Resources

1. Downgrade EC2 instances:
   - Change instance types from m5.large to t3.medium to match test workloads.
   - Savings: Approximately $150/month per instance.
2. Adjust RDS instance size:
   - Downgrade from db.m5.large to db.t3.micro for the test database.

Step 3: Optimize Storage

1. Enable S3 lifecycle policies:
   - o Move infrequently accessed logs to S3 Glacier.
   - o Set expiration policies for logs older than 90 days.
   - o Savings: Reduce storage costs by 80%.

Step 4: Leverage Spot Instances

1. Replace one EC2 instance with a Spot Instance for non-critical testing jobs.
   - o Savings: Up to 70% on instance costs.

Step 5: Implement Budgets and Alerts

1. Configure a budget in **AWS Budgets**:
   - o Set a monthly limit of $500 for the test environment.
   - o Receive alerts when spending exceeds 80% of the budget.

Outcome:

- Monthly costs for the test environment are reduced by 50% through right-sizing, storage optimization, and Spot Instances.

- The team maintains full functionality while staying within budget.

Effective cost management ensures that cloud resources are utilized efficiently, avoiding unnecessary expenses. Tools like AWS Cost Explorer, Azure Cost Management, and Google Cloud Billing provide actionable insights and optimization opportunities. Through the real-world example of reducing costs for a test environment, this chapter demonstrated practical steps to implement cost-saving strategies. In the next chapter, we'll explore hybrid and multi-cloud strategies, discussing how to leverage multiple cloud providers for flexibility and resilience.

CHAPTER 16: HYBRID AND MULTI-CLOUD STRATEGIES

Hybrid and multi-cloud strategies have become essential for businesses seeking flexibility, resilience, and scalability. These approaches allow organizations to combine on-premises infrastructure with cloud environments or leverage multiple cloud providers for specialized services. This chapter explores the benefits and challenges of hybrid and multi-cloud setups, highlights tools like AWS Outposts, Azure Arc, and Google Anthos, and provides a real-world example of integrating on-premises infrastructure with the cloud.

16.1 Benefits and Challenges of Hybrid and Multi-Cloud Environments

Benefits

1. **Flexibility**:
   - Utilize on-premises infrastructure for sensitive or latency-critical workloads while leveraging the cloud for scalability and innovation.

2. **Resilience**:
   - Avoid vendor lock-in by distributing workloads across multiple cloud providers.
   - Enhance disaster recovery options with diverse hosting locations.

3. **Cost Optimization**:
   - Keep predictable workloads on-premises while using the cloud for burst or temporary needs, reducing overall costs.

4. **Regulatory Compliance**:

      o Store sensitive data on-premises to meet compliance requirements while processing less-sensitive data in the cloud.

5. **Best-of-Breed Services**:

      o Access specialized services unique to each cloud provider, such as Google Cloud's AI/ML capabilities, AWS's compute options, or Azure's enterprise integrations.

Challenges

1. **Complexity**:

      o Managing multiple environments increases operational complexity and requires specialized expertise.

2. **Integration Issues**:

      o Ensuring seamless connectivity and interoperability between on-premises systems and multiple clouds can be challenging.

3. **Security and Compliance**:

      o Maintaining consistent security policies and compliance across environments requires robust governance.

4. **Cost Management**:

      o Monitoring and optimizing costs across multiple providers can be difficult without centralized tools.

5. **Data Transfer and Latency**:

   o Transferring data between on-premises systems and clouds or between clouds can introduce latency and incur additional costs.

16.2 Tools for Hybrid and Multi-Cloud Management

1. AWS Outposts

Overview:

AWS Outposts extends AWS services to on-premises environments, enabling consistent hybrid experiences.

Key Features:

- **Integrated Services**:
  o Access AWS compute, storage, and database services locally.
- **Consistent APIs**:
  o Use the same AWS APIs, tools, and workflows as the cloud environment.
- **Scalability**:
  o Seamlessly connect on-premises workloads to AWS cloud for scaling.

Use Cases:

- Low-latency applications.

- Data residency requirements.
- Running workloads locally while integrating with AWS cloud.

2. Azure Arc

Overview:

Azure Arc enables centralized management of hybrid and multi-cloud environments, extending Azure services to on-premises infrastructure and other clouds.

Key Features:

- **Unified Management**:
  - Manage Windows, Linux servers, Kubernetes clusters, and Azure services from a single interface.
- **Hybrid Cloud Integration**:
  - Deploy Azure SQL and Azure App Services on on-premises or other cloud platforms.
- **Policy Enforcement**:
  - Ensure consistent governance and compliance across environments.

Use Cases:

- Manage Kubernetes clusters across multiple clouds.
- Enable hybrid scenarios for applications requiring on-premises deployment.

3. Google Anthos

Overview:

Google Anthos is a platform for managing applications across hybrid and multi-cloud environments, with a focus on Kubernetes-based deployments.

Key Features:

- **Multi-Cloud Support**:
  - o Manage workloads on GCP, AWS, and on-premises systems.
- **Kubernetes-Native**:
  - o Provides consistent management for containerized applications.
- **Security**:
  - o Built-in security features like service mesh and policy enforcement.

Use Cases:

- Deploy and manage containerized applications across multiple clouds.
- Modernize legacy applications using Kubernetes.

Comparison of Tools

Feature	AWS Outposts	Azure Arc	Google Anthos
Hybrid Cloud Support	On-premises + AWS	On-premises + Azure + Multi-Cloud	On-premises + GCP + Multi-Cloud
Management Scope	AWS services	Servers, Kubernetes, databases	Kubernetes-based workloads
Use Cases	Low-latency workloads	Centralized hybrid management	Kubernetes application management
Strengths	Seamless AWS integration	Unified governance	Kubernetes and multi-cloud focus

16.3 Real-World Example: Combining On-Premises Infrastructure with Cloud

Scenario:

A healthcare organization needs to store sensitive patient data on-premises to comply with data residency regulations while leveraging the cloud for AI/ML analytics on anonymized data.

Solution Using Azure Arc

Step 1: Identify Workloads

1. **On-Premises Workloads**:
   o Patient records stored in a local SQL database.
2. **Cloud Workloads**:
   o AI/ML analytics using Azure Machine Learning on anonymized data.

Step 2: Deploy Azure Arc

1. Install the Azure Arc agent on the on-premises servers to onboard them into Azure.
2. Configure Azure SQL Managed Instance on the on-premises infrastructure for local data storage.

Step 3: Set Up Secure Data Transfers

1. Use **Azure Data Factory** to extract, transform, and load anonymized patient data into Azure cloud storage.
2. Implement encryption and access controls to secure data during transfer.

Step 4: Leverage Cloud for Analytics

1. Use Azure Machine Learning to train and deploy AI models on the anonymized dataset.
2. Store results in Azure Blob Storage for further analysis.

Step 5: Centralized Management and Governance

1. Use Azure Arc policies to enforce consistent security and compliance across both on-premises and cloud environments.
2. Monitor workloads using Azure Monitor, ensuring performance and security.

Outcome:

- The organization achieves compliance by storing sensitive data locally while leveraging the cloud's power for analytics.
- Centralized management via Azure Arc simplifies operations and ensures consistent governance.

Hybrid and multi-cloud strategies enable businesses to harness the best of both worlds, combining on-premises infrastructure with cloud services or leveraging multiple cloud providers for resilience and flexibility. Tools like AWS Outposts, Azure Arc, and Google Anthos simplify the management of hybrid and multi-cloud environments. Through the real-world example of integrating on-premises healthcare systems with Azure cloud analytics, this chapter demonstrated practical steps to implement a hybrid solution. In the next chapter, we'll explore the future of cloud computing, including trends like edge computing and serverless advancements.

CHAPTER 17: INTRODUCTION TO KUBERNETES

Kubernetes has revolutionized application deployment and management by providing a powerful framework for orchestrating containers. It automates deployment, scaling, and operations, enabling developers to focus on building applications instead of managing infrastructure. This chapter introduces Kubernetes basics, explores managed Kubernetes services like AWS EKS, Azure AKS, and Google Kubernetes Engine (GKE), and walks through deploying a containerized application.

17.1 Basics of Kubernetes and Container Orchestration

What Is Kubernetes?

Kubernetes (often abbreviated as K8s) is an open-source platform for automating the deployment, scaling, and management of containerized applications. Developed by Google, Kubernetes is now maintained by the Cloud Native Computing Foundation (CNCF).

Key Features of Kubernetes

1. **Container Orchestration**:
   - Manages the deployment, scaling, and networking of containers.
2. **Self-Healing**:
   - Automatically replaces or restarts failed containers.
3. **Load Balancing**:
   - Distributes traffic across multiple containers to ensure high availability.
4. **Scalability**:
   - Automatically scales applications based on resource usage or custom metrics.

5. **Declarative Configuration**:

   o Uses YAML or JSON manifests to define the desired state of applications and infrastructure.

6. **Multi-Cloud and Hybrid Support**:

   o Run Kubernetes clusters on-premises, in the cloud, or across multiple clouds.

Core Components of Kubernetes

1. **Cluster**:

   o A group of machines (nodes) managed by Kubernetes.

2. **Master Node (Control Plane)**:

   o Manages the cluster and schedules workloads on worker nodes.

   o Key components:

      ▪ **API Server**: Interface for communication with the cluster.

      ▪ **Scheduler**: Assigns workloads to nodes.

      ▪ **Controller Manager**: Ensures the desired state of resources.

      ▪ **etcd**: Stores cluster configuration data.

3. **Worker Nodes**:

   o Run the application workloads using containers.

   o Key components:

- **Kubelet**: Ensures containers are running as expected.
- **Kube-proxy**: Handles networking and load balancing.

4. **Pods**:
   o The smallest deployable unit in Kubernetes, typically representing a single container or a group of containers.

5. **Namespaces**:
   o Logical partitions within a cluster for resource isolation.

Why Use Kubernetes?

- **Efficiency**:
  o Optimizes resource utilization by scheduling containers based on resource needs.

- **Resilience**:
  o Provides built-in mechanisms for failover and recovery.

- **Portability**:
  o Standardizes deployment, making it easier to move applications across environments.

- **Ecosystem Support**:
  o Integrates with a wide range of tools for monitoring, logging, and CI/CD.

17.2 AWS EKS, Azure AKS, and Google Kubernetes Engine (GKE)

1. AWS Elastic Kubernetes Service (EKS)

Overview:

AWS EKS is a managed Kubernetes service that simplifies running Kubernetes clusters on AWS.

Key Features:

- **Integration**: Works seamlessly with AWS services like EC2, RDS, and IAM.
- **Scalability**: Supports Auto Scaling for both pods and nodes.
- **Managed Control Plane**: AWS manages the master nodes, ensuring high availability.

Use Cases:

- Microservices-based architectures.
- Hybrid applications using AWS Outposts.

2. Azure Kubernetes Service (AKS)

Overview:

Azure AKS provides a fully managed Kubernetes service with deep integration into the Azure ecosystem.

Key Features:

- **Cluster Autoscaler**: Automatically adjusts node pools based on demand.
- **DevOps Integration**: Works with Azure DevOps for CI/CD pipelines.
- **Security**: Integrated with Azure Active Directory for role-based access control (RBAC).

Use Cases:

- Enterprise applications requiring strong governance.
- Applications leveraging Azure-specific services like Azure Functions.

3. Google Kubernetes Engine (GKE)

Overview:

GKE is a managed Kubernetes service built on Google's infrastructure, offering advanced capabilities for container orchestration.

Key Features:

- **Auto-Pilot Mode**: Fully managed clusters with automated scaling and upgrades.
- **Global Load Balancing**: Distributes traffic across clusters in multiple regions.
- **Integrated Monitoring**: Built-in logging and monitoring via Google Cloud Operations Suite.

Use Cases:

- AI/ML workloads integrated with TensorFlow and BigQuery.
- Global applications requiring multi-region deployments.

Comparison of Managed Kubernetes Services

Feature	AWS EKS	Azure AKS	Google GKE
Control Plane Management	Fully managed	Fully managed	Fully managed
Integration	AWS ecosystem	Azure ecosystem	Google Cloud ecosystem
Scaling	Auto-scaling (nodes/pods)	Auto-scaling (nodes/pods)	Auto-scaling (nodes/pods)
Unique Strength	IAM and AWS service support	Azure DevOps and governance	Advanced auto-pilot features

17.3 Real-World Example: Deploying a Containerized Application

Scenario:

A retail company wants to deploy a containerized application for managing inventory. The application includes:

1. A backend API (Python Flask).
2. A frontend web application (React).
3. A MySQL database.

The company chooses **Google Kubernetes Engine (GKE)** for its advanced auto-pilot features and global availability.

Steps to Deploy
Step 1: Set Up GKE Cluster

1. Navigate to the Google Cloud Console.
2. Go to **Kubernetes Engine → Clusters**.
3. Click **Create Cluster** and choose:
   - **Cluster Type**: Auto-pilot.
   - **Region**: us-central1.
4. Click **Create** to launch the cluster.

Step 2: Create Kubernetes Manifests

1. Define the **frontend deployment**:

yaml

apiVersion: apps/v1
kind: Deployment

```yaml
metadata:
  name: frontend
spec:
  replicas: 3
  selector:
    matchLabels:
      app: frontend
  template:
    metadata:
      labels:
        app: frontend
    spec:
      containers:
      - name: react-app
        image: gcr.io/my-project/frontend:latest
        ports:
        - containerPort: 3000
```

2. Define the **backend deployment**:

yaml

```yaml
apiVersion: apps/v1
kind: Deployment
metadata:
  name: backend
```

```yaml
spec:
  replicas: 2
  selector:
    matchLabels:
      app: backend
  template:
    metadata:
      labels:
        app: backend
    spec:
      containers:
      - name: flask-api
        image: gcr.io/my-project/backend:latest
        ports:
        - containerPort: 5000
```

3. Define the **MySQL service**:

yaml

```yaml
apiVersion: v1
kind: Service
metadata:
  name: mysql
spec:
  type: ClusterIP
```

```
    selector:
      app: mysql
    ports:
    - protocol: TCP
      port: 3306
```

Step 3: Deploy Applications

1. Connect to the cluster using kubectl:

   bash

   ```bash
   gcloud container clusters get-credentials my-cluster --region us-central1
   ```

2. Apply manifests:

   bash

   ```bash
   kubectl apply -f frontend.yaml
   kubectl apply -f backend.yaml
   kubectl apply -f mysql.yaml
   ```

Step 4: Expose the Frontend

1. Create a LoadBalancer service for the frontend:

   yaml

```
apiVersion: v1
kind: Service
metadata:
  name: frontend-service
spec:
  type: LoadBalancer
  selector:
    app: frontend
  ports:
  - protocol: TCP
    port: 80
    targetPort: 3000
```

2. Apply the manifest:

bash

```
kubectl apply -f frontend-service.yaml
```

Step 5: Monitor and Scale

1. Use GKE's monitoring dashboard to view pod and cluster performance.

2. Enable auto-scaling for the backend:

bash

```
kubectl autoscale deployment backend --cpu-percent=70 --min=2 --max=5
```

Outcome:

- The application is deployed with high availability and scalability.
- GKE's monitoring tools ensure seamless operation, and auto-scaling adapts to workload fluctuations.

Kubernetes has become the de facto standard for orchestrating containerized applications, providing scalability, resilience, and portability. Managed services like AWS EKS, Azure AKS, and Google GKE simplify cluster management, allowing teams to focus on development. Through the real-world example of deploying a containerized application on GKE, this chapter demonstrated Kubernetes's power and flexibility. In the next chapter, we'll explore serverless container platforms and how they complement Kubernetes for specific use cases.

CHAPTER 18: ARTIFICIAL INTELLIGENCE AND MACHINE LEARNING

Artificial Intelligence (AI) and Machine Learning (ML) are transforming industries by enabling organizations to derive actionable insights from data, automate processes, and enhance customer experiences. Cloud platforms like AWS, Azure, and Google Cloud provide managed AI/ML services that simplify building, training, and deploying models. This chapter explores AI/ML services such as AWS SageMaker, Azure Machine Learning, and Google AI Platform, and walks through a real-world example of building a predictive model in the cloud.

18.1 AI/ML Services in the Cloud

1. AWS SageMaker

Overview:

Amazon SageMaker is a fully managed service that streamlines the process of building, training, and deploying machine learning models at scale.

Key Features:

- **Studio**:
    - An integrated development environment (IDE) for ML workflows.
- **Built-in Algorithms**:
    - Includes prebuilt algorithms like XGBoost, k-means clustering, and image classification.
- **Training and Hyperparameter Tuning**:
    - Automatically optimizes model parameters for better performance.
- **Model Deployment**:
    - One-click deployment of models with auto-scaling endpoints.
- **Integration**:
    - Seamlessly integrates with AWS services like S3, Lambda, and SageMaker Pipelines for MLOps.

Use Cases:

- Fraud detection in financial transactions.

- Predictive maintenance in manufacturing.

2. Azure Machine Learning

Overview:

Azure Machine Learning is a cloud service for training, deploying, and managing ML models, with a focus on operationalization and governance.

Key Features:

- **Automated ML**:
    - o Automates feature engineering and model selection.
- **Designer**:
    - o A drag-and-drop interface for building ML workflows without coding.
- **MLOps Integration**:
    - o CI/CD for ML models using Azure DevOps.
- **Compute Options**:
    - o Scales from local development to powerful GPUs and distributed clusters.
- **Explainability**:
    - o Built-in interpretability tools for model transparency.

Use Cases:

- Personalized recommendations in e-commerce.

- Sentiment analysis in social media data.

3. Google AI Platform

Overview:

Google AI Platform offers a robust ecosystem for developing and deploying machine learning models with the power of Google's infrastructure.

Key Features:

- **Pre-Trained APIs**:
    o Vision API, Natural Language API, and Speech-to-Text API for plug-and-play AI capabilities.
- **AI Platform Pipelines**:
    o Manages end-to-end ML workflows.
- **Custom Training**:
    o Supports TensorFlow, PyTorch, and scikit-learn for custom models.
- **BigQuery ML**:
    o Trains models directly in BigQuery using SQL.
- **AutoML**:
    o Automates training for structured and unstructured data.

Use Cases:

- Real-time translation with multilingual datasets.

- Image recognition for retail inventory management.

Comparison of AI/ML Services

Feature	AWS SageMaker	Azure Machine Learning	Google AI Platform
Model Training	Built-in algorithms	Automated ML and custom models	AutoML and custom frameworks
Deployment	Scalable endpoints	CI/CD pipelines	Kubernetes-based serving
Pre-Trained APIs	Limited	Moderate	Extensive (Vision, NLP, etc.)
Integration	AWS ecosystem	Azure ecosystem	Google Cloud ecosystem
Best Use Case	Scalability and flexibility	Operationalized ML workflows	AI-first workloads

18.2 Real-World Example: Building a Predictive Model in the Cloud

Scenario:

A retail company wants to predict product demand for the next month to optimize inventory management. The company has historical sales data, which includes:

1. Product ID.
2. Date of sale.
3. Quantity sold.
4. Store location.

The team decides to use **AWS SageMaker** for building and deploying the predictive model.

Steps to Build a Predictive Model

Step 1: Prepare the Data

1. Upload historical sales data to an S3 bucket in CSV format:
   - Bucket name: retail-sales-data.
2. Clean and preprocess the data:
   - Remove missing or invalid entries.
   - Aggregate daily sales data by product and location.

Step 2: Set Up SageMaker Studio

1. Open the SageMaker Console and launch **SageMaker Studio**.

2. Create a new Jupyter notebook and connect it to an instance with GPU support (e.g., ml.p3.2xlarge).

Step 3: Build the Model

1. Import required libraries:

python

```
import boto3
import pandas as pd
from sagemaker import Session
from sagemaker.xgboost import XGBoost
```

2. Load the dataset from S3:

python

```
s3 = boto3.client('s3')
bucket = 'retail-sales-data'
file_key = 'sales_data.csv'

response = s3.get_object(Bucket=bucket, Key=file_key)
sales_data = pd.read_csv(response['Body'])
```

3. Split the data into training and testing sets:

python

```python
from sklearn.model_selection import train_test_split

X = sales_data.drop(['Quantity'], axis=1)
y = sales_data['Quantity']

X_train, X_test, y_train, y_test = train_test_split(X, y, test_size=0.2)
```

4. Use SageMaker's built-in XGBoost algorithm for training:
   - Convert datasets to the format required by SageMaker:

   python

   ```python
   import sagemaker.inputs
   from sagemaker.amazon.amazon_estimator import get_image_uri

   train_data = pd.concat([y_train, X_train], axis=1)
   train_file = 'train.csv'
   train_data.to_csv(train_file,           index=False,
   header=False)

   s3.upload_file(train_file, bucket, 'train/train.csv')
   ```

```python
s3_train_uri = f's3://{bucket}/train/train.csv'
```

Step 4: Train the Model

1. Define the SageMaker training job:

python

```python
session = Session()
role = '<IAM role ARN>'
xgboost_container                              =
get_image_uri(session.boto_region_name, 'xgboost')

xgb = XGBoost(
    entry_point=None,
    framework_version='1.5-1',
    instance_type='ml.m5.large',
    output_path=f's3://{bucket}/output',
    role=role,
    sagemaker_session=session
)

xgb.fit({'train': s3_train_uri})
```

Step 5: Deploy the Model

1. Deploy the trained model as an endpoint:

python

```
predictor = xgb.deploy(
    initial_instance_count=1,
    instance_type='ml.m5.large'
)
```

2. Test the endpoint with sample data:

python

```
result = predictor.predict([[2024, 5, 'Product123',
'LocationA']])
print(result)
```

Step 6: Monitor and Optimize

1. Use SageMaker Model Monitor to track prediction accuracy.
2. Schedule retraining with updated sales data.

Outcome:

- The model predicts future demand for each product and location, enabling the retail company to optimize inventory levels.
- SageMaker's managed environment simplifies the end-to-end ML workflow, from training to deployment.

Cloud-based AI/ML services like AWS SageMaker, Azure Machine Learning, and Google AI Platform empower businesses to harness the power of machine learning without extensive infrastructure management. These services simplify data preparation, model training, and deployment while providing robust tools for scalability and monitoring. Through the real-world example of building a predictive model in SageMaker, this chapter demonstrated how cloud platforms can solve complex business challenges with ease. In the next chapter, we'll explore edge computing and its role in expanding cloud capabilities.

CHAPTER 19: BIG DATA AND ANALYTICS

Big data is transforming industries by enabling businesses to derive insights from massive volumes of structured and unstructured data. Cloud platforms provide powerful big data and analytics services, making it easier to store, process, and analyze data efficiently and at scale. This chapter introduces big data services such as AWS Redshift, Azure Synapse, and Google BigQuery, and walks through a real-world example of analyzing customer behavior using cloud analytics.

19.1 Big Data Services: Overview

1. AWS Redshift

Overview:

Amazon Redshift is a fully managed, petabyte-scale data warehouse that simplifies querying large datasets using SQL.

Key Features:

- **Massively Parallel Processing (MPP)**:
  - o Distributes query execution across multiple nodes for faster performance.
- **Data Lake Integration**:
  - o Seamlessly integrates with Amazon S3 for querying raw data.
- **Machine Learning**:
  - o Built-in ML capabilities to predict data trends directly within Redshift.
- **Scalability**:
  - o Supports on-demand and provisioned scaling.

Use Cases:

- Analyzing clickstream data for e-commerce platforms.
- Business intelligence dashboards.

2. Azure Synapse Analytics

Overview:

Azure Synapse is an analytics service that combines big data and data warehousing capabilities into a unified platform.

Key Features:

- **Unified Analytics**:
  - o Integrates SQL-based data warehousing with Spark-based big data processing.

- **Serverless Queries**:
  - o Analyze data in Azure Data Lake without provisioning infrastructure.
- **Tightly Integrated with Power BI**:
  - o Easily visualize and share insights.
- **Data Pipelines**:
  - o Built-in ETL tools for data integration and transformation.

Use Cases:

- Real-time fraud detection in financial systems.
- Large-scale reporting and analytics.

3. Google BigQuery

Overview:

Google BigQuery is a serverless, highly scalable data warehouse designed for fast SQL-based analytics on large datasets.

Key Features:

- **Serverless**:
  - o No need to manage infrastructure; scales automatically based on workload.
- **Real-Time Analytics**:
  - o Processes streaming data in near real-time.
- **BigQuery ML**:

    o Enables training and deploying ML models directly using SQL.

- **Integration**:
  - o Works seamlessly with Google services like Cloud Storage, Dataflow, and Looker.

Use Cases:

- Analyzing IoT sensor data.
- Marketing campaign performance analysis.

Comparison of Big Data Services

Feature	AWS Redshift	Azure Synapse Analytics	Google BigQuery
Data Storage	Columnar (optimized)	Unified storage and compute	Serverless columnar storage
Scalability	Provisioned or RA3 nodes	Elastic pools and serverless	Fully serverless
Machine Learning	Built-in ML capabilities	Integrated with Azure ML	BigQuery ML
Real-Time Analytics	Limited	Moderate	Strong (via streaming)

Feature	AWS Redshift	Azure Synapse Analytics	Google BigQuery
Integration	AWS ecosystem	Azure ecosystem	Google Cloud ecosystem

19.2 Real-World Example: Analyzing Customer Behavior Using Cloud Analytics

Scenario:

A retail company wants to analyze customer behavior to improve its online shopping experience. The goals are:

1. Identify popular products and seasonal trends.
2. Segment customers based on purchase patterns.
3. Recommend products based on customer interests.

The company chooses **Google BigQuery** for its serverless architecture and built-in machine learning capabilities.

Steps to Analyze Customer Behavior
Step 1: Prepare the Data

1. Consolidate data from various sources (e.g., website logs, transaction records) into **Google Cloud Storage**.
2. Organize data into the following files:

194

o transactions.csv: Customer purchases with columns like customer_id, product_id, amount, date.

o products.csv: Product details like product_id, category, price.

Step 2: Load Data into BigQuery

1. Open the **BigQuery Console**.
2. Create a new dataset named customer_behavior.
3. Load the CSV files into separate tables:

   o transactions and products.

Step 3: Query Data for Insights

1. **Identify Popular Products**:

   o Query to find the most purchased products:

   sql

   ```
   SELECT
     p.product_id,
     p.category,
     COUNT(t.product_id) AS purchase_count
   FROM
     `customer_behavior.transactions` t
   JOIN
     `customer_behavior.products` p
   ```

ON
  t.product_id = p.product_id
GROUP BY
  p.product_id, p.category
ORDER BY
  purchase_count DESC
LIMIT 10;

2. **Analyze Seasonal Trends**:
   o Query to analyze sales by month:

sql

```
SELECT
  EXTRACT(MONTH FROM t.date) AS month,
  SUM(t.amount) AS total_sales
FROM
  `customer_behavior.transactions` t
GROUP BY
  month
ORDER BY
  month;
```

3. **Segment Customers**:
   o Identify high-value customers based on total spending:

sql

```sql
SELECT
  customer_id,
  SUM(amount) AS total_spent
FROM
  `customer_behavior.transactions`
GROUP BY
  customer_id
ORDER BY
  total_spent DESC
LIMIT 10;
```

Step 4: Use BigQuery ML for Recommendations

1. **Train a Recommendation Model**:
   o Use BigQuery ML to train a matrix factorization model for personalized recommendations:

   sql

```sql
CREATE    OR    REPLACE    MODEL
`customer_behavior.recommendation_model`
OPTIONS(model_type='matrix_factorization')
AS
SELECT
  customer_id,
```

```
product_id,
COUNT(*) AS rating
FROM
`customer_behavior.transactions`
GROUP BY
customer_id, product_id;
```

2. **Generate Recommendations**:
   o Query to recommend products for a specific customer:

   sql

```
SELECT
 recommended_product
FROM
 ML.RECOMMENDATIONS(
   MODEL
`customer_behavior.recommendation_model`,
   STRUCT(123 AS customer_id)
 );
```

Step 5: Visualize Insights

1. Export query results to **Google Data Studio** for visualization.

2. Create dashboards showing:

   o Top products by category.

   o Monthly sales trends.

   o Customer segmentation.

Outcome:

- The retail company identifies top-selling products and peak sales periods.

- Customer segmentation helps target promotions to high-value customers.

- Personalized recommendations improve customer engagement and increase sales.

Big data and analytics services like AWS Redshift, Azure Synapse, and Google BigQuery empower organizations to analyze massive datasets and uncover actionable insights. These platforms provide scalable, efficient, and integrated tools for data storage and analysis. Through the real-world example of analyzing customer behavior with BigQuery, this chapter demonstrated how cloud analytics can drive business decisions and enhance customer experiences. In the next chapter, we'll explore cloud-native

DevOps practices for building, deploying, and maintaining applications.

CHAPTER 20: CLOUD MIGRATION

Migrating applications to the cloud is a transformative process that allows businesses to leverage the scalability, flexibility, and cost-efficiency of cloud platforms. However, migration requires careful planning and execution to minimize disruptions and maximize benefits. This chapter explores migration strategies, highlights tools like AWS Migration Hub, Azure Migrate, and Google Migration Center, and provides a real-world example of migrating a legacy application to the cloud.

20.1 Strategies for Migrating Applications to the Cloud

1. The 6 Rs of Cloud Migration

1. **Rehosting ("Lift and Shift"):**

- o Move applications as-is to the cloud without significant changes.
- o Pros: Quick and straightforward.
- o Cons: May not fully utilize cloud-native benefits.

2. **Replatforming ("Lift, Tinker, and Shift")**:
   - o Make minor optimizations to improve performance or reduce costs in the cloud.
   - o Example: Migrating a database to a managed service like Amazon RDS.

3. **Refactoring ("Re-Architecting")**:
   - o Redesign the application to be cloud-native.
   - o Pros: Maximizes scalability and efficiency.
   - o Cons: Requires significant time and effort.

4. **Repurchasing**:
   - o Replace the application with a SaaS solution.
   - o Example: Moving from on-premises CRM to Salesforce.

5. **Retiring**:
   - o Decommission obsolete or redundant applications.
   - o Pros: Reduces costs and complexity.

6. **Retaining ("Revisit Later")**:
   - o Keep certain applications on-premises due to technical or regulatory constraints.

2. Key Considerations

1. **Assessment**:
   - o Evaluate the application's architecture, dependencies, and performance requirements.
2. **Data Migration**:
   - o Plan for secure and efficient data transfer, considering size, format, and downtime.
3. **Security**:
   - o Implement identity, encryption, and compliance measures during and after migration.
4. **Testing**:
   - o Validate functionality and performance in the new environment.
5. **Optimization**:
   - o Post-migration, optimize for cost and performance using cloud-native features.

20.2 Migration Tools

1. AWS Migration Hub

Overview:

AWS Migration Hub provides a unified interface to track and manage migration projects across multiple AWS tools.

Key Features:

- **Discovery**:

- o Automatically assess on-premises workloads using tools like AWS Application Discovery Service.
- **Integration**:
  - o Supports migration tools such as AWS Database Migration Service (DMS) and Server Migration Service (SMS).
- **Tracking**:
  - o Provides a central dashboard to monitor migration progress.

Use Cases:

- Rehosting virtual machines (VMs) to EC2.
- Migrating databases to Amazon RDS or Aurora.

2. Azure Migrate

Overview:

Azure Migrate simplifies the assessment, migration, and modernization of workloads to Azure.

Key Features:

- **Comprehensive Assessment**:
  - o Evaluates VMs, databases, and applications for cloud readiness.
- **Integrated Tools**:

- o Works with tools like Azure Site Recovery and Database Migration Service.
- **Cost Estimation**:
  - o Provides cost projections for Azure resources.

Use Cases:

- Migrating on-premises Hyper-V or VMware VMs to Azure.
- Modernizing applications with Azure App Services.

3. Google Migration Center

Overview:

Google Migration Center provides tools for assessing and migrating workloads to Google Cloud.

Key Features:

- **Discovery and Assessment**:
  - o Analyzes workloads for cloud readiness and provides optimization recommendations.
- **Migration Automation**:
  - o Integrates with tools like Migrate for Compute Engine and Database Migration Service.
- **Sustainability Insights**:
  - o Evaluates the carbon footprint of migrations.

Use Cases:

- Migrating VMs to Google Compute Engine.
- Transitioning from proprietary databases to Cloud Spanner or BigQuery.

Comparison of Migration Tools

Feature	AWS Migration Hub	Azure Migrate	Google Migration Center
Discovery	Application Discovery Service	Built-in discovery tools	Built-in discovery tools
Tracking	Centralized dashboard	Comprehensive assessments	Centralized dashboard
Database Migration	DMS	Database Migration Service	Cloud SQL Migration Service
Unique Strength	Integration with AWS tools	Strong enterprise focus	Sustainability insights

20.3 Real-World Example: Migrating a Legacy Application to the Cloud

Scenario:

A manufacturing company runs a legacy inventory management application on an on-premises Windows Server. The company wants to migrate the application to the cloud to:

1. Reduce hardware maintenance costs.
2. Improve scalability.
3. Ensure data redundancy and disaster recovery.

The company chooses **Azure Migrate** for its comprehensive assessment and migration capabilities.

Steps to Migrate

Step 1: Assess the Existing Environment

1. Use **Azure Migrate Discovery and Assessment**:
   - Install the Azure Migrate appliance on the on-premises environment.
   - Discover the inventory management application and its dependencies.
   - Assess compatibility with Azure.

Assessment Results:

- The application and database are compatible with Azure Virtual Machines and Azure SQL Database.

- Suggested VM size: Standard_D4_v3 for optimal performance.

Step 2: Set Up Azure Environment

1. Create a resource group in Azure.
2. Configure a virtual network (VNet) for secure communication between the application and database.

Step 3: Migrate the Application

1. **Rehost the Application**:
   o Use Azure Migrate: Server Migration to migrate the on-premises VM to Azure.
   o Validate the application's functionality on the new VM.
2. **Migrate the Database**:
   o Use Azure Database Migration Service (DMS) to move the SQL Server database to Azure SQL Database.
   o Validate data integrity after migration.

Step 4: Configure and Test

1. **Network Security**:
   o Use Azure Firewall and Network Security Groups (NSGs) to secure the application.

2. **Load Balancing**:
   - Configure an Azure Load Balancer to distribute traffic across multiple instances.
3. **Testing**:
   - Perform end-to-end testing to ensure functionality and performance match or exceed on-premises levels.

Step 5: Optimize Post-Migration

1. Use Azure Advisor to identify cost-saving opportunities, such as resizing VMs.
2. Enable auto-scaling to handle variable workloads.

Outcome:

- The application operates reliably in Azure with reduced infrastructure costs.
- Azure SQL Database provides automated backups and high availability.
- The company achieves improved scalability and disaster recovery.

Cloud migration is a strategic process that allows organizations to modernize legacy systems, reduce costs, and improve scalability. Tools like AWS Migration Hub, Azure Migrate, and Google Migration Center simplify the migration journey, providing assessments, tracking, and automation. Through the real-world example of migrating a legacy inventory management application to Azure, this chapter demonstrated practical steps for successful cloud migration. In the next chapter, we'll explore cloud-native DevOps practices for building and maintaining applications in the cloud.

CHAPTER 21: DEVOPS IN THE CLOUD

DevOps practices focus on automating and improving collaboration between development and operations teams to streamline software delivery and infrastructure management. Cloud platforms provide tools that simplify Continuous Integration and Continuous Delivery (CI/CD), enabling teams to deploy applications faster and with fewer errors. This chapter explores cloud DevOps tools such as AWS CodePipeline, Azure DevOps, and Google Cloud Build, and demonstrates automating software deployment using a real-world example.

21.1 Cloud Tools for CI/CD

1. AWS CodePipeline

Overview:

AWS CodePipeline is a fully managed service that automates the CI/CD process for applications hosted on AWS.

Key Features:

- **Integration**:
  - Works with AWS services like CodeCommit, CodeDeploy, and S3, as well as external tools like GitHub.
- **Pipeline Stages**:
  - Supports build, test, and deploy stages with customizable workflows.
- **Version Control**:
  - Automatically triggers builds when changes are pushed to a repository.
- **Scalability**:
  - Handles pipelines for applications of any size.

Use Cases:

- Deploying containerized applications to Amazon ECS or EKS.
- Automating updates for serverless applications using AWS Lambda.

2. *Azure DevOps*

Overview:

Azure DevOps is a suite of tools for managing and automating CI/CD pipelines, project tracking, and collaboration.

Key Features:

- **Azure Pipelines**:
    - Fully automated CI/CD pipelines with support for multi-cloud and hybrid environments.
- **Integration**:
    - Works with GitHub, Bitbucket, and Azure Repos for version control.
- **Infrastructure as Code**:
    - Automates provisioning using tools like Terraform and Azure Resource Manager (ARM).
- **Built-In Testing**:
    - Supports automated unit and integration testing during CI/CD.

Use Cases:

- Deploying applications to Azure App Services, Kubernetes, or Virtual Machines.
- Managing end-to-end workflows for software delivery.

3. *Google Cloud Build*

Overview:

Google Cloud Build is a serverless CI/CD platform for building, testing, and deploying applications on Google Cloud or other environments.

Key Features:

- **Serverless**:
  - No infrastructure to manage, scales automatically with workloads.
- **Custom Build Steps**:
  - Use prebuilt or custom build steps defined in a YAML configuration file.
- **Artifact Registry**:
  - Stores and manages container images and build artifacts.
- **Integration**:
  - Integrates with Google Kubernetes Engine (GKE), App Engine, and Firebase.

Use Cases:

- Building and deploying containerized applications.
- Automating deployment for mobile and web applications.

Comparison of Cloud DevOps Tools

Feature	AWS CodePipeline	Azure DevOps	Google Cloud Build
Deployment Targets	AWS Services	Azure and hybrid clouds	Google Cloud and Kubernetes
Version Control	CodeCommit, GitHub	Azure Repos, GitHub	Cloud Source Repositories
Build Automation	CodeBuild	Azure Pipelines	Built-in
Best Use Case	AWS-centric workflows	Enterprise-level projects	Containerized applications

21.2 Real-World Example: Automating Software Deployment Using Cloud DevOps

Scenario:

A fintech company wants to automate the deployment of its web application to a Kubernetes cluster on Google Kubernetes Engine (GKE). The application is stored in a GitHub repository and requires automated testing, containerization, and deployment to staging and production environments.

The company selects **Google Cloud Build** for its serverless CI/CD capabilities.

Steps to Automate Deployment

Step 1: Prepare the Environment

1. **Set Up GKE Cluster**:
   - Create a Kubernetes cluster in Google Cloud:

   bash

   ```
   gcloud container clusters create web-app-cluster --num-nodes=3 --region=us-central1
   ```

2. **Configure Kubernetes Context**:
   - Authenticate the kubectl command-line tool:

   bash

   ```
   gcloud container clusters get-credentials web-app-cluster --region=us-central1
   ```

Step 2: Define the Cloud Build Pipeline

1. **Create a cloudbuild.yaml File**:
   - Define the pipeline stages for building, testing, and deploying the application:

```yaml
yaml

steps:
- name: 'gcr.io/cloud-builders/docker'
  args: ['build', '-t', 'gcr.io/$PROJECT_ID/web-app:$COMMIT_SHA', '.']

- name: 'gcr.io/cloud-builders/docker'
  args: ['push', 'gcr.io/$PROJECT_ID/web-app:$COMMIT_SHA']

- name: 'gcr.io/cloud-builders/kubectl'
  args:
  - 'set'
  - 'image'
  - 'deployment/web-app'
  - 'web-app=gcr.io/$PROJECT_ID/web-app:$COMMIT_SHA'
  env:
  - 'CLOUDSDK_COMPUTE_ZONE=us-central1-a'
  - 'CLOUDSDK_CONTAINER_CLUSTER=web-app-cluster'

images:
```

```
- 'gcr.io/$PROJECT_ID/web-app:$COMMIT_SHA'
```

2. **Upload the Configuration File**:
   o Commit the cloudbuild.yaml file to the GitHub repository.

Step 3: Connect GitHub to Cloud Build

1. **Enable Cloud Build Triggers**:
   o In the Google Cloud Console, go to **Cloud Build →**
     Triggers.
   o Create a new trigger that listens to changes in the GitHub repository.
2. **Configure the Trigger**:
   o Trigger type: Push to the main branch.
   o Build configuration: Use the cloudbuild.yaml file.

Step 4: Test the Pipeline

1. **Push Changes to GitHub**:
   o Make a change to the application code and push to the main branch:

   bash

   git add .
   git commit -m "Updated web app"

```
git push origin main
```

2. **Monitor the Build**:
   - Open the Cloud Build dashboard to track the build progress.

Step 5: Deploy to Staging and Production

1. **Staging Deployment**:
   - Configure a Kubernetes namespace for staging:

   bash

   ```
   kubectl create namespace staging
   kubectl apply -f k8s/deployment-staging.yaml
   ```

2. **Production Deployment**:
   - After successful testing, promote the build to production:

   bash

   ```
   kubectl apply -f k8s/deployment-production.yaml
   ```

Step 6: Monitor and Optimize

1. **Enable Logging**:
   - o Use Google Cloud Logging to monitor the application's logs.
2. **Set Up Alerts**:
   - o Configure alerts for failed builds or deployment issues.

Outcome:

- The web application is automatically built, tested, and deployed to GKE upon code changes.
- Developers can focus on building features, knowing deployments are reliable and automated.
- The CI/CD pipeline ensures consistent and error-free releases across staging and production.

Cloud DevOps tools like AWS CodePipeline, Azure DevOps, and Google Cloud Build empower organizations to automate and streamline software delivery processes. These tools integrate seamlessly with their respective cloud ecosystems, enabling efficient CI/CD workflows. Through the real-world example of automating a Kubernetes-based deployment using Google Cloud Build, this chapter demonstrated the power and practicality of cloud-native DevOps practices. In the next chapter, we'll explore edge computing and how it complements cloud computing for low-latency and distributed applications.

CHAPTER 22: INDUSTRY USE CASES

Cloud computing has become a cornerstone for digital transformation across industries, enabling organizations to enhance efficiency, scalability, and innovation. This chapter explores how industries such as healthcare, finance, and education adopt cloud technologies to solve unique challenges. It also highlights real-world case studies that demonstrate how leading organizations leverage cloud services to achieve their goals.

22.1 Cloud Adoption Across Industries

1. Healthcare

Cloud adoption in healthcare focuses on improving patient care, ensuring data security, and enabling innovative solutions such as telemedicine and predictive analytics.

Key Applications:

- **Electronic Health Records (EHRs):**

- o Centralized cloud-based systems provide easy access to patient data for healthcare providers.
- **Telemedicine**:
  - o Platforms like AWS Chime and Azure Communication Services enable remote consultations.
- **Predictive Analytics**:
  - o Machine learning models on platforms like Google AI Platform predict patient outcomes and optimize resource allocation.

Challenges:

- Ensuring compliance with regulations like HIPAA and GDPR.
- Maintaining patient data privacy and security.

Example:

- **Mayo Clinic** uses Google Cloud to power its advanced clinical analytics, improving patient outcomes through AI-driven insights.

2. Finance

Financial institutions leverage the cloud for real-time transaction processing, fraud detection, and enhanced customer experiences.

Key Applications:

- **Real-Time Processing**:
  - o Platforms like AWS Lambda and Azure Functions enable instant payment processing.
- **Fraud Detection**:
  - o AI services like Amazon Fraud Detector identify suspicious transactions.
- **Risk Management**:
  - o Big data services like Azure Synapse Analytics calculate risk in real-time.

Challenges:

- Meeting stringent regulatory requirements (e.g., PCI DSS, SOX).
- Ensuring data sovereignty and preventing cyberattacks.

Example:

- **Capital One** moved its operations entirely to AWS, achieving greater scalability, enhanced security, and faster innovation cycles.

3. Education

The education sector uses cloud platforms to enhance learning experiences, enable remote education, and manage institutional operations.

Key Applications:

- **Remote Learning**:
  - Platforms like Google Classroom leverage Google Cloud to deliver seamless virtual classrooms.
- **Student Analytics**:
  - Cloud-based data analytics help track student performance and personalize learning.
- **Administrative Efficiency**:
  - SaaS solutions like Microsoft Dynamics improve resource management.

Challenges:

- Bridging the digital divide for underprivileged students.
- Securing student data while complying with regulations like FERPA.

Example:

- **Arizona State University (ASU)** uses AWS to deliver adaptive learning experiences, improving student engagement and success rates.

22.2 Real-World Case Studies

Case Study 1: Healthcare – Moderna's Vaccine Development
Problem:

- Moderna needed to accelerate vaccine development during the COVID-19 pandemic by managing vast amounts of genomic data.

Solution:

- **AWS**:
  - Moderna used AWS Lambda for real-time genomic data processing.
  - Amazon S3 provided secure, scalable storage for sensitive research data.
  - AWS's High-Performance Computing (HPC) clusters powered simulations and analytics.

Outcome:

- Reduced time for vaccine candidate selection from months to weeks.
- Enabled global collaboration between research teams.

Case Study 2: Finance – Nasdaq's Market Data Platform
Problem:

- Nasdaq needed to process and analyze large volumes of market data in real time for traders worldwide.

Solution:

- **Google Cloud**:
  - BigQuery enabled real-time analysis of market data.
  - Pub/Sub handled real-time messaging for high-frequency trading platforms.
  - Cloud Spanner provided a globally consistent database for transactional data.

Outcome:

- Delivered analytics to customers in sub-second timeframes.
- Enhanced platform reliability and scalability to handle market fluctuations.

Case Study 3: Education – Coursera's Global Learning Platform
Problem:

- Coursera needed to scale its platform to support millions of students globally, especially during the pandemic-driven demand surge.

Solution:

- **Azure**:

- o Azure Kubernetes Service (AKS) scaled containerized applications to meet demand.
- o Azure Content Delivery Network (CDN) optimized video delivery to students worldwide.
- o Azure Machine Learning personalized course recommendations.

Outcome:

- Achieved a 300% increase in user capacity without service disruptions.
- Delivered personalized learning experiences, increasing course completion rates by 20%.

Cloud computing has revolutionized industries by enabling solutions that improve efficiency, scalability, and innovation. Healthcare uses cloud platforms for patient care and predictive analytics, finance leverages the cloud for real-time processing and fraud detection, and education adopts cloud technologies for remote learning and personalized education. Through real-world examples such as Moderna, Nasdaq, and Coursera, this chapter demonstrated how leading organizations utilize cloud services to achieve transformative outcomes. In the next chapter, we'll explore emerging trends in cloud computing, including edge computing, serverless advancements, and quantum cloud services.

CHAPTER 23: THE FUTURE OF CLOUD COMPUTING

Cloud computing continues to evolve rapidly, reshaping industries and introducing new paradigms in technology. Emerging trends like edge computing, quantum computing, and sustainability initiatives are driving innovation, while major cloud providers like AWS, Azure, and Google Cloud expand their capabilities to address future challenges. This chapter explores these trends, predicts future developments, and offers guidance on how developers can prepare for the evolving landscape.

23.1 Emerging Trends in Cloud Computing

1. Edge Computing

Overview:

Edge computing moves data processing closer to the source of data generation, reducing latency and improving real-time performance. This paradigm is particularly relevant for applications requiring low-latency processing, such as IoT, autonomous vehicles, and AR/VR.

Key Features:

- **Decentralized Processing**:
  - o Data is processed on devices or edge nodes instead of centralized data centers.
- **Improved Latency**:
  - o Reduces the delay in data transmission for time-sensitive tasks.
- **Integration with Cloud**:
  - o Often works in tandem with cloud platforms for data storage and analytics.

Examples:

- AWS IoT Greengrass: Extends AWS services to edge devices.
- Azure IoT Edge: Deploys AI and analytics on edge devices.
- Google Distributed Cloud: Processes data locally with tight integration into Google Cloud.

2. Quantum Computing

Overview:

Quantum computing uses quantum mechanics to solve problems that are infeasible for classical computers. While still in its infancy, cloud providers are making quantum computing accessible through cloud-based platforms.

Key Features:

- **Exponential Speed**:
    - Tackles problems like cryptography, material science, and optimization.
- **Hybrid Models**:
    - Combines classical and quantum computing for practical applications.
- **Cloud Integration**:
    - Accessible via cloud platforms for experimentation and development.

Examples:

- Amazon Braket: Provides a development environment for quantum algorithms.
- Azure Quantum: Offers tools for quantum development with hardware integration.
- Google Quantum AI: Focused on quantum research and applications.

3. Sustainability in the Cloud

Overview:

Sustainability is becoming a core focus for cloud providers as businesses aim to reduce their carbon footprint. Cloud platforms are optimizing energy usage, leveraging renewable energy, and introducing tools to monitor sustainability.

Key Features:

- **Carbon-Neutral Goals**:
  - ○ Providers are committing to net-zero carbon emissions.
- **Energy Efficiency**:
  - ○ Innovations like liquid cooling and custom chips reduce energy consumption.
- **Sustainability Tools**:
  - ○ Cloud dashboards provide insights into energy usage and emissions.

Examples:

- AWS Sustainability Pillar: Helps organizations design energy-efficient architectures.
- Microsoft Sustainability Calculator: Tracks carbon emissions across Azure services.
- Google Cloud Carbon Footprint: Monitors emissions tied to cloud usage.

23.2 Predictions for AWS, Azure, and Google Cloud

1. AWS

- **Enhanced AI and ML Integration**:
  - ○ AWS is likely to deepen its AI/ML services, offering prebuilt models for specific industries like healthcare and finance.

- **Edge Expansion**:
  - o Increased investment in AWS Outposts and Local Zones to support edge computing.
- **Quantum Innovation**:
  - o Expansion of Amazon Braket with new quantum hardware and hybrid quantum-classical capabilities.

2. Azure

- **Focus on Enterprise Solutions**:
  - o Azure will continue dominating hybrid cloud scenarios, integrating tools like Azure Arc and Synapse Analytics for large enterprises.
- **Quantum for Businesses**:
  - o Azure Quantum will offer practical tools for optimization and simulation problems.
- **AI-Powered Governance**:
  - o Advanced AI tools for managing compliance and governance in multi-cloud environments.

3. Google Cloud

- **AI-First Approach**:
  - o Google Cloud will lead in AI-driven services, offering advancements in BigQuery ML, AutoML, and Vertex AI.
- **Edge and IoT Leadership**:

- o Google Distributed Cloud will focus on 5G-enabled IoT applications and low-latency workloads.
- **Sustainability Leadership**:
  - o Enhanced sustainability metrics and renewable energy initiatives to maintain its carbon-neutral leadership.

23.3 How Developers Can Prepare for the Future

1. Master Cloud-Native Technologies

- **Containers and Kubernetes**:
  - o Learn tools like Docker and Kubernetes to deploy scalable, cloud-native applications.
- **Serverless Architectures**:
  - o Explore serverless services like AWS Lambda, Azure Functions, and Google Cloud Functions for cost-efficient computing.

2. Embrace AI and ML

- **AI/ML Frameworks**:
  - o Gain proficiency in TensorFlow, PyTorch, or scikit-learn for developing AI models.
- **Cloud ML Services**:

- o Use AWS SageMaker, Azure Machine Learning, or Google AI Platform to streamline model development and deployment.

3. Develop Edge and IoT Expertise

- **IoT Platforms**:
  - o Experiment with AWS IoT Core, Azure IoT Hub, and Google IoT Core.
- **Edge Development**:
  - o Build and deploy edge applications using tools like AWS Greengrass and Azure IoT Edge.

4. Explore Quantum Computing

- **Basics of Quantum**:
  - o Learn foundational concepts like qubits, entanglement, and quantum gates.
- **Cloud-Based Quantum Platforms**:
  - o Experiment with Amazon Braket, Azure Quantum, and Google Quantum AI for hands-on experience.

5. Focus on Sustainability

- **Green Cloud Design**:

- o Design architectures that minimize energy consumption and leverage renewable-powered regions.
- **Sustainability Metrics**:
  - o Use tools like Google Cloud Carbon Footprint to track and optimize energy usage.

The future of cloud computing is shaped by innovations like edge computing, quantum computing, and sustainability. AWS, Azure, and Google Cloud are driving these advancements, enabling businesses to solve complex problems and adopt environmentally conscious practices. By mastering cloud-native technologies, AI/ML tools, and emerging paradigms like quantum computing, developers can stay ahead in this dynamic field. This chapter highlights how embracing these trends equips organizations and professionals to thrive in the evolving cloud landscape.

www.ingramcontent.com/pod-product-compliance
Lightning Source LLC
LaVergne TN
LVHW051321050326
832903LV00031B/3300